DATE DUE

BRODART   Cat. No. 23-221

Two Hearts, One Soul

Two Hearts, One Soul

The Correspondence of the
Condesa de Galve,

1688–96

Edited, annotated, and translated by
Meredith D. Dodge   Rick Hendricks

University of New Mexico Press
Albuquerque

Library of Congress Cataloging-in-
Publication Data

Galve, Gelvira de Toledo, condesa de, 17th cent.
[Correspondence. English and Spanish.
Selections]
Two hearts, one soul : the correspondence of
the Condesa de Galve, 1688-96 / edited, annotat-
ed, and translated by Meredith D. Dodge,
Rick Hendricks. p. cm.
Translations of the letters, addressed chiefly to
the Marqués del Cenete, later known as the
Duque del Infantado, which are now in the
Archivo Histórico Nacional, in Madrid, in the
Sección de Osuna, legajos 89 and 239.
"The poetry of Sor Juana Inés de la Cruz" (p.
163-178) contains the texts of poems dedicated to
the Condesa de Galve.
"Spanish transcripts" (p. 187-232) contains the
original texts of the letters.
Includes bibliographical references.
ISBN 0-8263-1419-8
1. Galve, Gelvira de Toledo, condesa de,
17th cent.-Correspondence.
2. Viceroy's wives—Mexico—Correspondence.
3. Infantado, Gregorio de Silva y Mendoza,
duque del, 1649-1693-Correspondence.
4. Mexico—History—Spanish colony,
1540 -1810.
5. Cerda Sandoval Silva y Mendoza, Gaspar de
la, conde de Galve, 1653-1697.
6. Mexico—Social life and customs.
7. Spain—Social life and customs—
17th century.
I. Dodge, Meredith D., 1950-.
II. Hendricks, Rick, 1956-.
III. Infantado, Gregorlo de Silva y Mendoza,
duque del, 1649-1693.
IV. Juana Inés de la Cruz, Sister, 1651-1695.
Poems. Selections. 1993.
V. Title.
F1231.G1713 1993
972'.02'092—dc20   92-36895
CIP

Library of Congress Cataloging-in-
Publication Data

Galve, Gelvira de Toledo, condesa de, siglo XVII
[Correspondencia. Español e inglés.
Selecciones]
Dos corazones, una alma: la correspondencia de la
condesa de Galve, 1688-96/ editada, anotada y tra-
ducida por Meredith D. Dodge,
Rick Hendricks. p. cm.
Traducción de las cartas dirigidas principalmente
al marqués del Cenete, conocido posteriormente
como el duque del Infantado, las cuales se encuen-
tran ahora en el Archivo Histórico Nacional de
Madrid, Sección de Osuna, legajos 89 y 239.
"La poesía de Sor Juana Inés de la Cruz" (p. 163-
178) contiene los textos de los poemas
dedicados a la condesa de Galve.
"Transcripciones en español" (p. 187-232) contiene
los textos de las cartas originales. Incluye referen-
cias bibliográficas.
ISBN 0-8263-1419-8
1. Galve, Gelvira de Toledo, condesa de,
siglo XVII —Correspondencia.
2. Esposas del virrey—México—Correspondencia.
3. Infantado, Gregorio de Silva y Mendoza, duque
del, 1649-1693—Correspondencia.
4. México—Historia—colonia española,
1540-1810.
5. Cerda Sandoval Silva y Mendoza,
Gaspar de la, conde de Galve, 1653-1697.
6. México—vida social y costumbres.
7. España—vida social y costumbres—
siglo XVII.
I. Dodge, Meredith D., 1950-
II. Hendricks, Rick, 1956- .
III. Infantado, Gregorio de Silva y
Mendoza, duque del, 1649-1693.
IV. Juan Inés de la Cruz, hermana, 1651-1695.
Poemas. Selecciones. 1993.
V. Título
F1231.G1713 1993
972' .02'092—dc20   92-36895
CIP

IV

For Μήμη *and Lois*

CONTENTS

FOREWORD

A number of contemporary works posit a crisis in early modern European history. Perry Anderson's *Lineages of the Absolutist State*, Geoffrey Parker's *Europe in Crisis, 1598-1648*, V.G. Kiernan's *State and Society in Europe, 1550-1650*, R.A. Stradling's *Europe and the Decline of Spain*, and Trevor Aston's *Crisis in Europe, 1560-1660* amply analyze European society in the throes of new religious, military, social, and economic pressures, a time of "refeudalization," religious and imperial warfare, severe economic change, and social regression.

Spain, by virtue of its imperial and Hapsburg identity, stood at the apex of this crisis, a Great Power on its way to oblivion, to paraphrase Paul Kennedy. Yet for all the attention paid to this Spanish crisis, the society of this century has remained remarkably faceless. Professor John Elliott's Olivares is the only figure to emerge from obscurity in the first half of the seventeenth century, and there are none for the second half, at least until now, with this study of the letters of Gelvira de Toledo, the Condesa de Galve.

Olivares and Gelvira, of course, are figures of a society at different ends of the spectrum—one, *the* statesman of the time, a major figure, his life found in the documents of the 1620s and 1630s; the other, wife of a viceroy of New Spain, indistinct, buried by role and gender on the other side of the world from Europe. Nevertheless, knowing something about the Condesa de Galve opens a small window on a period we know so little about and is akin to the excitement felt twenty years ago as Elliott's life of Olivares unfolded.

The most remarkable aspect about this small volume is its focus on a woman about whom previously nothing was known.

FOREWORD

Biographies of Spanish women are almost nonexistent; in the period from 1450 to 1650, Queen Isabel, Santa Teresa, and Sor Juana Inés de la Cruz are the only exceptions to anonymity, but just barely. Impact of the early modern crisis upon the social history of Spanish women is even less well known, especially in English-language studies. Historians believe that a great loss of prerogative and status for women followed the Council of Trent (1545–63), as if they alone were expected to bear the brunt of Counter Reformation changes; but what these changes were and to what degree greater religious severity influenced behavior, dress, attitude, and a whole host of other questions has never been looked at until now.

So it is refreshing to read something of the life of doña Gelvira and try to understand the veiled and complicated psychology of a late seventeenth-century Spanish woman whose life and experience spanned peninsular and imperial society—a vantage point of extreme importance.

This is an unusually gifted book, carried out by two skilled young historians who already have more archival experience than most scholars achieve in a lifetime.

Robert W. Kern
Professor of Iberian History
University of New Mexico

A Note on Editorial Methods

Few collections of personal correspondence from seventeenth-century Spain and New Spain exist. Of those that do, most are written by men. We are publishing here, in English translation, twenty-seven letters written by Gelvira de Toledo, the Condesa de Galve, to family and friends in Spain. A few letters, the addressees of which we were unable to identify, have not been included in this volume.

The letters are found in the Archivo Histórico Nacional in Madrid, Spain, in the Sección de Osuna in Legajos 89 and 239. They are part of a larger collection, numbering more than four thousand legajos, that originally made up the family archive of the House of Osuna. The AHN permanently acquired the collection in 1927, when an anonymous benefactor generously provided for its purchase.

In some respects, it seems remarkable that the collection has survived at all. Most of the communication, much of a very intimate nature, is directed to her brother-in-law, Gregorio de Silva y Mendoza, the Marqués del Cenete and Duque de Pastrana (later Infantado). In almost any other context than that of the nobility of the seventeenth century, such epistles would surely prove a deep family embarrassment.

We may never really know the character of their relationship, a harmless episode of *amor cortés,* or courtly love, or a truly forbidden passion. This is never revealed.

What we do see in her letters is something of the daily life of a noble Spanish woman of her time and a great deal of her inner thoughts and feelings as expressed through her words. In an era when we are beginning to hear more clearly the authentic voice of the other, Gelvira is almost wholly in line with the stereotype of the seventeenth-century Spanish woman, almost frustratingly so. To complement her own observations, we have addressed the socioeconomic and cultural milieu in which she lived in the first of two interpretive essays. The first essay precedes the thirteen letters written in Spain.

Gelvira is more forthcoming about life around her in the viceregal capital, Mexico City. Nevertheless, she does not provide sufficient detail to paint a portrait of her life as the vicereine of New Spain. By relying on a contemporary diarist, Antonio de Robles, for a chronology, it was possible to recreate much of her day-to-day activities in a second essay, which introduces the fourteen New World letters.

The lack of biographical details pertaining to Gelvira's life underscores the difficulty of producing women's history, even for women of the elite. Fortunately, a dissertation on the social history of Galve's administration of New Spain will soon appear as part of the Colección Virrey Mendoza de Guadalajara. It will probably contain additional biographical information bearing on Gelvira's personal life.

In translating these letters, we have tried to serve two masters: historical accuracy and Gelvira's unique, individual voice. Her language is usually simple and direct, but can be idiomatic and expressive as well; we have taken every care to render it consistently into readable English. We have supplied paragraphing, punctuation, and specific nouns where distant or unclear antecedents may cause confusion. We have modernized names in the text with the single exception of Gelvira's. While in modern

Spanish the name would be spelled Elvira, we have chosen to leave it exactly as she wrote it. For those students of language and literature who may find them of interest, semipaleographic transcriptions of the original Spanish letters have been provided in Appendix 4.

Our basic reference for place-names is *Webster's New Geographical Dictionary,* and our authority on spelling is *Webster's Third New International Dictionary of the English Language Unabridged.* The names of Spanish kings and noble titles are retained in Spanish. Offices or military titles are abbreviated when they appear with the person's given name and spelled out when only the surname occurs. Saints, names are given in their Spanish forms, especially when part of churches, corporate bodies, or places.

We can only hope we have done doña Gelvira justice. If her letters teach us "something about a woman's life" in imperial Spain, she deserves the credit. We the editors accept the responsibility for any mistakes.

Abbreviations

AL   Autograph letter
ALS Autograph letter signed
L   Letter
LS   Letter signed

The World of doña Gelvira

Doña Gelvira de Toledo's world was a Spain of diminished circumstances and national disappointment. The waning years of Habsburg Spain revealed a country beset by economic collapse, a fumbling foreign policy, and political ineptitude and corruption. Close upon the reigns of Carlos V (1517–56) and Felipe II (1556–98), periods characterized by the brilliance of empire and world hegemony, came the indifferent rule of Felipe III (1598–1621), the intermittently effective government of Felipe IV (1621–65), and, finally, the disaster of Carlos II (1665–1700). While many of Castile's problems during Carlos's monarchy were inherited, the later seventeenth century also witnessed a complex of infelicitous conditions that marked the certain decline of a once-great power.

In the external sphere, defense and foreign policy were more attuned to the sixteenth-century imperial ideals of world hegemony and militant Catholicism than to the stark realities of the seventeenth.[1] The seemingly interminable war with the Netherlands, which was resumed in 1621, represented the most significant drain on Spain's resources. The struggle to retain the heretic Dutch rebels within the Habsburg fold had begun in 1556. Over time, the rebellion demanded ever-higher claims on Castilian revenues and manpower that were increasingly difficult for an impoverished Spain to provide.[2] When peace finally came with the Treaty of the Pyrenees in 1659, it signified that Spanish political will had at last succumbed to the exhausted state that its financial resources had reached years before.

Another of Spain's prized European holdings, the Italian territories, was also problematic. The governments of Naples and

Sicily had always proved highly lucrative for the governors and viceroys posted to them, and the corrupt manipulation and cooptation of local elites had spawned their share of resentment. Revolts in 1647 and 1674 were indications not only of continued disaffection, but also of French interest in fomenting anti-Spanish feeling whenever and wherever possible.[3]

France contributed to many of Spain's foreign and domestic problems, a mark of its increasing world power. Just as the sixteenth century had belonged to Spain, the seventeenth was to be France's. Having survived Protestant revolts in the late 1620s and the civil wars of the Fronde from 1648 to 1655, France was well placed by midcentury to supplant Spanish hegemony in Europe. Early in the absolutist reign of Louis XIV (1643–1715), Cardinal Mazarin (1602–61) concluded the Treaty of the Pyrenees (1659). This pact ended twenty-four years of Franco-Spanish conflict and the threat of France's encirclement by the Habsburgs. It also formalized the betrothal of Felipe IV's elder daughter, María Teresa, to Louis XIV. This treaty marked the emergence of France as the ruler of Europe's destiny[4]

France's growing superiority had been foreshadowed a generation earlier when it attempted to influence two critical internal events in Spain, the revolt of Catalonia and the succession to the Portuguese throne. Resistance to increasing political and financial pressure from Madrid led the Catalans, with France's encouragement and subsequent support, to open revolt in 1640. Portugal, in reluctant union with Spain since 1580, followed Catalonia's lead, initiating a struggle for independence that was enthusiastically supported by France. While Catalonia made its peace with Madrid in

1652, the Luso-Hispanic war dragged on until 1668, when an exhausted Spain accepted the inevitable and recognized Portuguese sovereignty.[5]

These events provided an inauspicious beginning for Carlos II's reign. Upon the death of Felipe IV in 1665, the government of Spain initially fell to Queen Mariana (1634–96) as regent, with a junta de gobierno, or advisory council, to assist her. Under Mariana's inept rule, Spain endured a bleak time. Her reign was characterized by political corruption in an atmosphere of growing aristocratic reaction that would have been unthinkable during the period of Felipe IV's reign. First came a military coup establishing a government that lasted into the early years of Carlos's kingship. When Carlos's illegitimate half-brother, don Juan de Austria (1629–79), assumed de facto leadership in 1669, there seemed some hope that he might be able to effect the reforms the country so desperately needed. His unexpected death in 1679, however, merely opened the way to the machinations of political adventurer Fernando de Valenzuela (1636–92), Mariana's favorite. By the time Carlos reached his majority in 1675, it was clear that the ship of state was hopelessly adrift.[6]

Unfortunately for Spain, Carlos II fell far short of being the man of the hour. Chronically infirm, he proved incapable of providing the strong leadership the circumstances required. As the weakness of the monarchy was revealed, traditional government through the conciliar system became moribund. Politics, however, did not. Political life in Madrid now centered on the personality of the valido, or royal favorite, and lapsed into the worst kind of factionalism along the lines of house and family. Spanish nobles exercised their dominance in a scramble to acquire wealth and favor. Unable to live on their own means, they were now true pensioners of the crown. Forsaking their earlier responsibility to provide military support for the government, the nobility increasingly led a life of indulgence and intrigue, in large part financed by the crown, which could ill afford it.[7]

Had foreign interference in Spain's internal affairs been the only danger Madrid faced, perhaps a solution to its increasingly imperiled national integrity could have been fashioned. Spain's dire economic situation, however, posed a far more serious, and long-standing, threat to the country, one capable of rending it asunder.

The root of most of Spain's problems in the seventeenth century was its unstable economy, particularly in the years after 1625, when inflation of Castile's vellon currency began to reach disturbing levels.[8] In the early seventeenth century, as silver remissions from the Indies began to diminish, the crown increasingly resorted to minting copper vellon for use within Castile. The result was to inflate the economy, which led to the flight of silver to foreign creditors and trading partners, rapid fluctuations in prices, the appearance of counterfeit money, and a growing disparity between wages and prices.[9]

Unstable finances, and a lack of political will to remedy them in a conscientious manner, led the crown to desperate, though ineffective, measures. By midcentury, the government was increasingly employing juros, or bonds, to convert its short- and medium-term debt to the longer term. Private silver remittances from the Indies were seized, and their unhappy owners compensated with bonds, the government's pledge of eventual repayment. This was done despite full knowledge that state revenues were pledged so far into the future, and the collection of revenues so uncertain because of the poor state of the economy, that full reimbursement was unlikely. Government bankruptcies, tactically employed since 1557, were declared five times in the century. Manipulation of the vellon currency, including artificial raising of value and forced official deflations such as those of 1642, 1652, 1664, and 1680, added to the financial chaos.[10]

Coupled with the refusal to undertake the painful economic reforms necessary to save the economy was a series of crippling natural disasters. Severe fluctuations in climate throughout the century had an adverse impact on agriculture. Crop losses, particularly in Andalusia, began the century and reached critical levels in the 1670s and 1680s. Years of heavy rain alternated with years of drought to destroy grain and cattle throughout the southern and middle regions of Spain. Inevitably, high prices for foodstuffs, and sometimes famine, followed these losses, particularly in the late 1670s. Epidemic disease accompanied these climatological disasters throughout the century. The first widespread episode occurred from 1597 to 1602. Sweeping from north to south, it may have killed more than half a million people. Catastrophic outbreaks between 1647 and 1654 in some places, such as Seville, took as much as half the population. A final wave, lasting from 1676 to 1685, was less virulent, but more persistent.[11]

Agricultural failures and disease had a devastating effect on the population, but they were not the only negative influences. The expulsion of the Moriscos from 1609 to 1614, which had an uncertain impact in Castile, meant the loss of an economically significant population in southeastern Spain. Further, immigration to the Indies continued to drain manpower from the peninsula. War, so much a feature of the seventeenth century, also played a role in consuming manpower that could have been more usefully employed elsewhere.[12]

The resulting drop in population in turn had a deadly impact on the economy, especially in agriculture. Early on, perhaps as much as 30 percent of the unskilled labor force was lost. Adding to this was a general flight from rural to urban areas in an attempt to escape the brutal living conditions of the countryside. Over the course of the century, these twin phenomena led to a gradual depopulation of the agricultural areas of Castile and a concomitant concentration of land, as landowners moved to usurp deserted communal lands.[13]

The economic consequences of inflation, famine, and rising prices were unequally felt in Spanish society. The middle and, especially, the lower classes bore the brunt of an economy gone wrong, while the increasingly urban nobility managed to maintain a comparatively luxurious style of life. In the midst of want, the nobility supported large households in Madrid, a practice reflecting both the linkage of nobility and largess and the custom of keeping on existing retainers upon inheritance of a house. They were abetted by the crown in this, both indirectly and directly. The crown had a long-standing policy of supporting the retention of family wealth through the institution of *mayorazgos*, or entailed estates, by which the core of a family's wealth was entailed and could only be alienated with royal permission.[14] A more straightforward form of assistance, and one that became increasingly employed in the seventeenth century, was crown provision to the nobility of the financial means that permitted them to lead a privileged way of life. Whether in the form of elevated political positions, such as viceroyalties, or cash grants in the form of living expenses, nobles managed to accumulate the resources necessary to supplement their heavily mortgaged fortunes and live beyond their actual means.[15] In this sense, they were merely following the lead of the royal family, which saw its household expenses almost double from around 1 million escudos in the early years of Felipe IV's reign to 1,812,989 in the later years of Carlos II's.[16]

The nobility's parasitic and costly way of life was not, however, a concern in the seventeenth century. In a society as hierarchical, status conscious, and patriarchal as Castile's, the elite were the cultural arbiters, setting the standards in all aspects of life. The nobility was best placed to live out ideas concerning personal honor, purity of blood, the importance of family ties, and the centrality of the Catholic faith, but these values permeated society at all levels. Even the basest agricultural laborer brooked no slur against his reputation.[17]

The cultural unanimity these shared values reflected was nowhere clearer than in the ideas expressed regarding women and their proper role in Spanish society. Three fundamental concepts are noteworthy about this mindset. First, these ideas were largely male-defined. This is not to imply that women had no input into the ideological structure that shaped their lives and behavior, but such ideas were male expressions of ideal feminine comportment they hoped to, and did, elicit.[18] Second, although it is impossible to quantify, most women probably supported and believed in such ideas themselves. It should not be surprising that people living in an established cultural milieu were thoroughly imbued and acted in accord with the prevailing values of their time. The truly unusual was the rare, iconoclastic woman who sought to challenge such beliefs, which is why a Sor Juana Inés de la Cruz stood out in such bold relief. Third, the positive idealized norms supported by Spanish culture necessarily found expression primarily among elite women. Characteristics valued in feminine behavior—modesty, obedience, seclusion, chastity, moderation, and fidelity among others—could only be fully acted upon by women who had both means and opportunity. Most women, burdened with caring for family and home or worse, lacking male protection and support, were in no position to live out prescribed standards that strongly emphasized women's seclusion. Like their elite counterparts, however, they too bore the weight of negative stereotypes that portrayed women as weak, prone to error, gossipy, deceitful, and profligate.

Religious writers had produced a well-developed literature defining desirable and objectionable behaviors for women by the late sixteenth century. Augustinian theologian and poet fray Luis de León's *La perfecta casada* (1583), one of the most widely distributed books in Spain, continued to be a customary gift from a fiancé to his betrothed into the next century.[19] The list of virtues was formidable: foremost among them was female confinement to the home, particularly for young, unmarried, and presumably vulnerable, women.[20] Gaspar de Astete, a Jesuit moral philosopher, was firm on this point, stating that one of the most laudable characteristics a woman could have was to willingly accept seclusion. This was necessary, because women, in public and left to their own devices, would lapse into sin, particularly since they were weak by nature. Parents also needed to be careful about those they employed in the household; a young woman could easily be corrupted by servants.[21]

Confinement to the home implied close supervision of a young woman's activities and education. Instruction in the domestic arts was strongly emphasized, but anachronistic. Moralists counseled the teaching of cooking, sewing, spinning, weaving, and embroidery. These skills, though, were inappropriate at a time when, because of depressed economic conditions, servants were readily available to the middle and upper classes and finished goods were easily bought.[22] These suggestions seemed more directed to ensuring that women had something, no matter how trivial, to occupy their every moment. The horror of female idleness was a constant theme.

Astete praised the young woman who, while under her parents' roof, served them in all things, no matter how base, and made herself as their slave.[23] He seemed particularly suspicious of married women with time on their hands. He wrote that among the signal virtues a married woman could possess was love for and attraction to work. He cited the chaste Penelope, who wove, and then unraveled her weaving, to keep herself occupied during Ulysses's absence. Women should "rise early, work, and retire late," thereby devoting close attention to every domestic detail.[24]

Instruction was not necessarily limited to the domestic arts, above all in the case of elite women. Although in general the moralists frowned on instruction in singing, dancing, the playing of instruments, and recitation, Astete, for one, thought this permissible, provided it took place within the confines of the home under careful parental supervision. Privileged women were frequently schooled in these social graces, without which a well-bred woman might not be considered acceptable for marriage.[25]

Any discussion of what constituted the appropriate content of women's instruction was subsumed in the larger question of whether women should be educated at all. Erasmus (1469?–1536) broached the subject early and was a particularly progressive voice. He endorsed no particular course of studies for women, but placed no limit—within Christian boundaries—on acceptable subject matter, even suggesting that women could be taught Latin and Greek. His only admonition was that education should not be an alternative to domestic pursuits, but an enhancement of them, and that women should make no public display of their knowledge. The purpose of education was to produce a woman better able to watch over her household and give proper guidance to her children.[26]

Juan Luis Vives, as befitted an intellectual companion of the scholarly Catherine of Aragon, followed this humanist current and espoused educating women to the limit of their intellectual capacity. Most other moralist writers viewed such liberality with grave reservations.[27] In *La perfecta casada,* León stated the case most fundamentally by arguing women's natural intellectual inferiority. Because women possessed only limited understanding, they were incapable of treating matters of substance. God had circumscribed both their power of reasoning and means of expression, which was as it should be. Their roles in life as helpmate to husband and manager of the home and family demanded no more.[28]

Astete agreed with his fellow writers that a woman's primary virtues should be charity, obedience, silence, seclusion, and chastity. He wrote, however, that parents could teach their daughters to read. This was an honest and praiseworthy use of time, but care should be taken that instruction remained in the hands of relatives or trustworthy retainers and always within the home.[29] He parted company with León in his uncharacteristic belief that women were not by nature intellectually inferior to men. It was justification enough for women to learn to read if their native intelligence, their virtue and healthy desire to improve themselves, their need to administer family matters, or their intention to enter conventual life made it necessary.[30]

Reading had as its corollary the bothersome question of the advisability of teaching women to write. While some usefulness could be discerned in women acquiring the ability to express themselves in writing, to the sixteenth- and seventeenth-century male mind, it was fraught with peril. Written self-expression presented opportunities for women to circumvent their male-enforced seclusion by communicating directly, though not in person, with individuals outside the home; conniving servants were thought to abet women in this deceit. The great fear, of course, was that these individuals would be male, and the moralists' imaginations predicted the lurid illicit consequences that would result from women breaking free from the confinement men wished upon them.[31]

Limited approval of women's learning to read brought with it the question of what constituted appropriate reading material.[32] Opinion was fairly uniform on this matter, but the works encompassed an impressively wide range. Women were to be directed to uplifting material that would encourage the development of chaste love and socially approved female virtues.[33] Vives's recommendations included the Old Testament, and in the New, the Acts of the Apostles and the Epistles. Certain of the classical prosaists and poets, such as Plato, Seneca, and Cicero, were allowed, as were St. Jerome, St. Augustine, St. Gregory, and St. Catherine of Siena.[34] Astete, who accepted devotional and scriptural texts without qualification, expanded the list to include secular works. Greek and Latin histories, particularly those of Caesar, Livy, and Virgil, were all commendable if read in the original. Should a woman be untutored in Latin or Greek, histories of the church, the chronicles of Spain, and even those of the conquest of the Indies could be profitably read, since they inspired prudence, good judgment, strength of character, and love of virtue.[35]

A fairly tolerant agreement on what was permissible to read was transformed into a rigid certainty when the question of what was unsuitable came under discussion. The purpose of reading was edification and self-improvement. Devotional books, wrote Astete, were as the purest mirrors, in which one could, through reflection and comparison, discover one's flaws and thereby work to rectify them.[36] For this reason, women and men alike were to be prevented at all costs from reading novels of courtly love and romances of chivalry. Such works, filled with pleasant words, were replete with lies that corrupted the soul. They incited unseemly thoughts and inflamed desires inappropriate in a Christian woman. Tears wasted for a fictional knight dead in battle or the failed advances of an unsuccessful suitor could not later be shed in contemplation of one's sins or Christ's bitter passion.[37]

These writings were overtly pernicious, but also damnable

because of their insidious nature. Once read, their vain and sinful contents lodged perpetually in the mind, to be cast out only when acted upon. Such were the dangers of these works that the only definitive safeguard against them was to consign them to the flames: "If she wishes to save her soul, she should burn dishonest books, so that she will not burn with them in hell forever."[38]

Some measure of the ire this literature aroused is evidenced in Astete's description of its authors. In a paroxysm of condemnation, he wrote that they were "liars . . . whose mouths are full of evil, blasphemies, and obscenity; whose throats are as fetid graves, emitting decay and stench; whose hearts are beds of corruption of complete wickedness."[39]

While such denunciations indicated, if indirectly, that novels of courtly love still maintained passionate appeal among their female audience, the stridency of the objections seemed disproportionate.[40] In fact, the moralists' concern was well placed, since the literary ideals of courtly love promoted a radically subversive model of behavior directly opposed to the male-defined standards of conduct deemed appropriate for women.

Intimate relations between men and women, whether within the context of kinship, marriage, or the church, were predicated upon male domination and guidance of women. The necessity of this arrangement was firmly rooted in Catholic theology. Because Eve condemned all humankind by partaking of the Tree of Knowledge, women, fragile and prone to error, could be expected to sin as a matter of course.[41] This perceived inability to control behavior led forthwith to what society defined as the cardinal female virtue: obedience to father, brother, husband, and confessor.

Courtly love contradicted this norm in two ways. First, it posited a role reversal whereby a supplicant male pursued a seemingly unavailable and certainly inappropriate woman, tailoring his actions to satisfy the whims, however unreasonable, of the object of his desire. In this situation, the woman became the figure of power and the shaper of relations, the controller, rather than the controlled.

Second, inherent in the concept of courtly love was the erotic component of passion and the possibility of the mortal sin of adultery. Although this relationship was usually portrayed in ideal and platonic terms, thereby evading the question of sexual sin, consummation was never categorically excluded, nor matrimony necessarily expected. It would be difficult to conceive a more fundamental affront to the seventeenth-century concept of male honor, which was so firmly rooted in protection of and belief in the integrity of female chastity.

Herein, then, lies the source of the moralists' rage over the literature of courtly love and the obvious attraction such a concept would have for women. In contradistinction to norms of female seclusion from the world, male control, and parental choice of spouse, novels of chivalry permitted and even encouraged the unleashing of eroticism and the expression of female sexual identity outside the confines of marriage.[42]

The enormous appeal of these ideas in the seventeenth century, furthermore, was not merely theoretical. A ritualized form of flirting and courtship, the *galanteo,* was a prominent feature of life among the elite, fueled not only by the fantasies promoted by literature, but also by their well-known, though privately conducted, propensity to libertine behavior.[43] So prevalent was this licentiousness that foreign travelers noted that upper-class men who lacked lovers were considered unmanly. The crown went so far as to attempt to ban the galanteo.[44]

Further evidence of the relaxed mores and comportment of the aristocracy, particularly among women, comes, again, from the pens of the moralists. They railed unsuccessfully against women's excessive use of cosmetics and personal adornment, seeing in them the means to incite men's carnality. Women usually applied their makeup twice daily, on arising and on retiring; it was used so heavily that the skin underneath could not be seen. To darken eyebrows and eyelashes, women coated them with antimony, while substances were used both to whiten the skin of the face and to add color to cheeks, chin, throat, ears, shoulders, and hands. When greeting one another, women shook hands rather than kissing cheeks, so as to avoid smearing their cosmetics. Liberally applied makeup was an affront to God, for it was an attempt to improve upon, or disguise, His handiwork.[45]

Proper female dress was also a sore point. Women of the upper class lived up to the lowest expectations of the moralists. Waist-cinching corsets, in a culture that worshipped the slender female form, were the norm, and women bound their breasts in order to appear flat-chested. Necklines revealed the throat, shoulders, and a good part of the breasts. Very high heels, although dangerous to walk in, augmented height. Women were able to turn this hazard to their advantage, though, by using the occasion of a twisted ankle to pass notes to their suitors. The exaggerated hoop skirt, a particular favorite of the young Queen Mariana of Austria, had passed out of fashion by the end of Felipe IV's reign. These were particularly objectionable, because a woman could hide a pregnancy under their voluminous folds. Women wore attractive clothing primarily to draw attention to themselves with the aim of entrapping men in sensual love. They were unceasing in their demands that their husbands or lovers satisfy their appetite for adornment, wheedling and whining until they had their way. Expenditures for such finery was further proof of their poor judgment and spendthrift natures. Clothing should be the outward manifestation of the inner woman, or, as León stated, it was not enough to be chaste; one had to appear so as well.[46]

On no topic, however, were the moralist writers more strident, and more prolific, than on the subject of marital fidelity and adultery, and rightly so, for this struck at the very heart of Spain's male-dominated society. While rates of infidelity are impossible to ascertain with certainty, the amount of verbiage expended on the phenomenon, and Spain's elevated level of illegitimacy, indicate it was common enough.[47]

The seventeenth-century obsession with adultery, and its corollary, male honor, was prevalent among all classes. Members of the elite, because of the greater freedom their social standing afforded, were no doubt in a better position to act upon their desires. Nonetheless, adulterous women and men were judged by different standards. Francisco de Osuna advanced the most basic argument for this in the 1540s when he wrote that unequal treatment was justified because "we are men and you women; we are masters and you servants; we are the head and you the limbs. . . . Human laws punish the evil of the husband less in this case than that of women. . . .Judges do not believe women when they accuse their husbands of being adulterers and say they do not believe them because they present a suspicion as a certainty. I, however, think they do not believe because as there are nearly innumerable adulterous husbands, all the judges would be occupied in sentencing them. . . ."[48]

Condemnation of women's adultery was universal among the moralists for both theoretical and practical reasons. At the most fundamental level, and reflecting how deeply misogyny permeated Spanish society, adultery violated natural laws, upsetting the very order of the cosmos. As León wrote in 1583, "As a woman violates her husband's trust, so the stars lose their light, the heavens fall, the laws of nature are broken, and everything returns to that first and ancient confusion." Although both spouses had a duty to be faithful, because women were considered to belong to men, they could not give themselves to another. In the event they did, the resulting offense to male honor arose from the woman's act of depriving the male of something to which she had no right.[49] Furthermore, adultery was an offense against a sacrament instituted by God, and one He intended to reflect the purity and joy of the heaven in which it was created. Adulterers who rebelled against His wish brought an indelible stain to a marriage, while the ensuing discord transformed it into hell on earth.[50]

Because the fundamental inequality of the sexes was an acknowledged fact, there could simply be no excuse for a woman straying outside marriage. Schooled to be obedient to males, and viewed as fatally flawed morally, no woman could justify infidelity and turning her back on her husband's honor no matter what the provocation.[51] Adultery was also against the law. By her very actions, an adulterous woman mocked the laws of her country. Flagrant disrespect for her nation's institutions reflected her scorn for her nation itself, a very grave offense indeed.[52]

On a more mundane level, adultery was wrong because of the complications it introduced into questions of inheritance and property. A wife's fidelity was the only guarantee a man had that he was the father of his children. Aside from the cuckolding—an insult to male honor—the incorporation of another man's offspring into the home caused a great injustice, since property would eventually pass to those not entitled to it.[53]

Punishment for adulterous behavior also varied according to gender, and, in the case of women, was left in the hands of the offended male partner. The thirteenth-century *Fuero juzgo* and later codes all permitted, but did not mandate, a husband killing an unfaithful wife or wayward daughter if caught flagrante delicto. He could also dispatch the unfortunate partner with impunity. Mere suspicion, followed by denunciation to the authorities and clear proof of transgression, resulted in a wife's being returned to her husband for execution or pardon. The patent unfairness of these provisions, or, perhaps, the twinge of Christian conscience, induced moralist writers to soften their attitudes somewhat. While all supported the existence of such laws, and the code of honor that underlay them, they opposed death for women found guilty of adultery.[54]

The coexistence of a proscriptive morality carefully circumscribing female behavior in general and condemning female adultery in particular and an ideology of courtly love that women found interesting and attractive described the dilemma elite seventeenth-century Spanish women faced. Flirting and courtship were indulged and perhaps even expected of women. Within limits, the acting out of these social roles was permitted. Penalties, often terrible ones, awaited women who sought to defy societal standards through unconventional behavior. It is therefore little wonder that they chose to do what was expected of them, both in terms of class and gender. To do otherwise was to astonish.

It is in this light that the attitudes and behavior of doña Gelvira de Toledo, as far as they can be discerned in her correspondence, must be viewed. Although a woman of some education, as her letters witness, she seemed content to fulfill the preconceptions about a woman of her class and time. She was in every respect a living stereotype, the epitome of all the moralists dreaded. Even what might be viewed as her single rebellious act, maintaining an illicit correspondence with her adored brother-in-law, conformed to moralists' expectations. In her early writing, there are glimpses of the fair lady clearly under the influence of the ideals of courtly love. Repeated expressions of undying desire are directed to her knight in the hope of reciprocation. By turns coquettish and importuning, she embodied the very characteristics moralist writers warned women to eschew. Her later correspondence, decidedly more temperate, reveals a woman who took her marital responsibilities seriously, but one who understood the circumscribed world to which her interests were socially confined. Matters of family, health, and the household were her primary concern, but her manner is now embued with a sense of decorum befitting the matron of a great viceregal house.

The World of doña Gelvira

Although her letters are in some respects intensely personal, doña Gelvira as a historical figure remains elusive. This is not, on the one hand, surprising, considering the obstacles inherent in researching women's history. On the other, it is, for of the *grandeza*, the twenty or so most prominent families of Spain, few could claim as illustrious a genealogy as that of her family, the Toledos, or her husband's, the Silva y Mendozas.

The extended Toledo clan claimed a long and prestigious record of service to king and empire. In the direct line, Fadrique de Toledo, doña Gelvira's paternal grandfather, was one of the most outstanding naval figures of his age, at a time when it was increasingly unfashionable for the nobility to pursue military careers. Felipe III appointed him Captain General of the Ocean Sea in 1618. Further honors came in 1624, when he was granted the title of Marqués de Villanueva de Valdueza, and in 1628, when Felipe IV named him Captain General of the kingdom of Portugal and Comendador of the Order of Santiago. He achieved his fullest prominence in the 1620s and 1630s, winning both great popular acclaim and the implacable enmity of the Conde-Duque de Olivares (1587–1645), Spain's leading statesman. A victory over a superior Dutch fleet in the Straits of Gibraltar in 1621 was followed by command of the Luso-Spanish fleet dispatched in February 1625 to recover Pernambuco. On 1 May of that year, the twelve-thousand-man, fifty-two-ship fleet forced a Dutch surrender in Brazil.

In 1634, he requested permission to remain in Spain in order to attend to his long-neglected affairs. Olivares's ever-increasing jealousy over Toledo's status as a national hero secured denial of this request and appointment to the command of yet another fleet to Brazil. When Toledo attempted to refuse the posting, Olivares had him arrested and imprisoned outside Madrid.

Toledo, who had fallen ill, suffered further humiliation when, in the autumn, the Council of Castile sentenced him to perpetual exile from Castile, the loss of all his offices and the income from his estates, and a fine of 10,000 ducats. Only the intercession of his wife, Elvira Ponce de León, with Queen Mariana spared him the indignity of learning of the council's decision before his death in December.[55]

This unsavory incident had no lasting effect on the family's fortunes, for Gelvira's father, also named Fadrique, went on to match his father's preeminence. Upon the death of his uncle, García de Toledo Osorio, also a noted naval commander, Fadrique inherited his title, becoming the seventh Marqués de Villafranca and the third Duque de Fernandina; he also retained his father's title as the second Marqués de Villanueva de Valdueza. A member of the Order of Santiago, he served both as comendador of Valde-Ricote, one of the Order's estates, and as a *trece*, one of the thirteen officials appointed for the Order's General Chapter. He also held a knighthood in the Italian Order of the Holy Spirit.

His government service was wide ranging, encompassing both military and civilian postings. He served as viceroy of Sicily and captain general of the Naples galleys. On his return to Spain, he sat on the Councils of State and War. He held the post of gentleman of the chamber in Carlos II's household and ended his career as senior majordomo for Felipe V, finally dying in 1705.[56]

In the early 1650s, he wed María Manuela Francisca de Jesús Fernández de Córdova Cardona y Aragón. Baptized on 1

January 1634, she was the daughter of Antonio Francisco Fernández de Córdova, the seventh Duque de Sessa and ninth Conde de Cabra, and his wife, Teresa Pimentel y Ponce de León, both grandees. In a time of very high infant mortality, Fadrique and María were fortunate to produce six offspring, all of whom survived to adulthood: José, Antonio, Luis, Francisco Melchor, Teresa, and Gelvira.[57]

Doña Gelvira's marriage to Gaspar Melchor Baltasar de Silva Sandoval y Mendoza took place between 1685 and 1686. The match was a favored one, for if her family was one of Spain's most prominent, his was truly first among equals. Gaspar was the youngest child save one and, by the death of his older brother Francisco, second son of Rodrigo de Silva y Mendoza, the Duque de Pastrana and, through his marriage to Catalina Gómez de Sandoval y Mendoza, eighth Duque del Infantado.[58]

By the time the Infantado title came to Rodrigo in 1657 through the premature death of doña Catalina's brother, Rodrigo Díaz de Vivar Sandoval y Mendoza, he was already a well-known figure in Madrid. Dividing his time among residences at Guadalajara, Pastrana, and the capital, as a young man he was strongly attracted by the social diversions court life offered. An ambitious, litigious figure, and something of a dandy, Rodrigo's joining of the Pastrana and Infantado titles made him the object of envy in court circles.[59]

Not all was frivolity, however, for Rodrigo proved eager to avail himself of the rewards life at court held. In 1639, he was mentioned as a candidate for the Viceroyalty of Aragon, though he did not receive the appointment. He did not accept an offer of the governorship of Oran in north Africa in 1643, probably because he lacked the requisite military experience. These missed opportunities presented no obstacle to his reception of royal largess. In 1654, he was appointed guarda mayor for the Monte de la Seca in Medina del Campo. Later that same year, he was given the right to hold multiple city council seats in Toledo, Segovia, Valladolid, Guadalajara, and Tordesillas, a prestigious, though illegal, royal gift. He was also perpetual warden of the fortresses of Simancas and Tordesillas. His gratitude for such generosity was demonstrated by his raising six infantry companies for Felipe IV in 1657.[60]

A wealthy man in his own right, but reputed to be greedy and close with a ducat, Rodrigo was the master of extensive properties in Spain and Italy. By the mid-1650s, he enjoyed an annual income of more than 60,000 ducados. Shortly after assuming the Infantado title, he moved his family permanently to Madrid and took up residence in his mother's houses there. Nevertheless, he was soon rudely disabused of any notion he may have entertained about increasing his fortunes by inheritance of the Infantado title. Only eight months after relocating to Madrid, he returned to his estates, telling doña Catalina that he could not support the family in the capital and that everything about the Infantado title was a sham.[61]

The joys of family life did not compensate for dissatisfaction with the economic circumstances of the House of Infantado. After doña Catalina and Rodrigo's marriage in 1630, six children arrived, but only four survived into adulthood. Leonor, born in 1636, became a Discalced Carmelite over her father's strong objections; she died at the age of twenty-three. Juan María lived only five months, and as a consequence of his death, Gregorio, born in 1649, became the first-born son and heir to the Infantado title. Gaspar, born in 1653 in Pastrana, was the second son. José María, the youngest, was born in 1654. Carlos II named him the first Marqués de Melgar in 1676, but he held the title only six years before his death.[62]

Gregorio spent his childhood in Pastrana and Madrid, where some properties of the Infantado family bordered on those of the Marqués de Villafranca, Gelvira's father. He matured into an attractive, urbane man. At seventeen, he married the lovely María de Haro y Guzmán, daughter of the deceased Luis Méndez de Haro y Guzmán y Sotomayor, the sixth Marqués del Carpio, and Catalina Fernández de Córdoba y Aragón. The couple produced ten children, boys and girls equally, but only five achieved maturity: María Teresa, Catalina María, Luisa María, Juan de Dios, and Manuel María José. Juan later inherited the Infantado title from his father, while Manuel, upon the death of his uncle Gaspar, became the Conde de Galve.[63]

Favor came early to Gregorio. The year of his marriage, he became comendador of the Encomienda Mayor of Castile in the Order of Santiago. A year later, he received a company of the Castilian Guards. In 1674, he was appointed royal huntsman and gentleman of the chamber for Carlos II. As a result of his father's death that same year, he assumed his title as Duque de Pastrana. His formal reception into the grandeza came in 1676, along with his mayorazgo and his mother's transfer to him of the wardenship of Simancas.[64] In 1677, Gregorio had the honor of accompanying Carlos II's royal progress to Aragon, where he attended the king's public entry into Saragossa on 1 May. This foreshadowed his prominent role in the elaborate preparations for the marriage between Carlos II and María Luisa de Orléans (1662–89) of France. In 1679, he was chosen by Carlos as ambassador extraordinary to present the royal marriage jewels to the French princess. After securing a 100,000-ducado loan against his mayorazgo to finance his mission, Gregorio journeyed to France in the company of his younger brothers Gaspar and José. The French court afforded him a resplendent reception. After his return to Spain, he participated in María Luisa's entrada in Madrid in January 1680.[65]

The 1680s brought further prestige. In 1686, Gregorio became the Duque del Infantado following his mother's death in July. The decade also saw his yet more intimate association with the palace. In 1688, he was appointed royal chamberlain and took up residence in the palace. He sat on the Council of State, serving coincidentally at the same time as Gelvira's father. Carlos II awarded him the treasured Toisón de Oro in May 1693, but his rise to the heights of power ended abruptly with his death in September in his living quarters in the palace. The cosmopolitan courtier died as he had lived, close to the remnants of power in the capital of a moribund empire.[66]

As the second son, Gaspar could perforce never hope to eclipse his brother's accomplishments, and, to judge by his early years, it appeared that he would remain unmarked by greatness. Yet, the strong and loving friendship Gregorio and Gaspar forged in their youth lasted a lifetime and was unmarred by sibling rivalry or petty jealousy. Gaspar seemed content in his role as the younger brother, sharing in, but never surpassing, Gregorio's eminence.[67] Gaspar's early career is unremarked, beyond the fact that he was a royal page to Queen Mariana. In 1675, he became one of Carlos II's gentlemen of the bedchamber, but only with right of entrance. The full privileges associated with the position, which Gregorio already enjoyed, did not come until 1677. His father's death in 1675 brought him his mayorazgo of Sacedón and Tortola and other revenues worth more than 35,000 ducados a year, as well as a council seat in Guadalajara and wardenship of León's castle. His inheritance increased in 1677 when he received from the estate of his great-grandfather, the Duque de Lerma (1550?–1625), another mayorazgo comprising 15,000 ducados, wardenship of the fortress of Toledo, and the tercias reales of Ampudia.[68]

The next year saw his induction into the Order of Alcántara, not the most prestigious military order, Santiago, of which his brother was a member. It did bring with it, however, the revenues associated with the Order's encomienda of Ceclavín.

In 1673, he had already received the right to future succession in Salamea, another of the Order's holdings; full possession came in 1682.[69]

At twenty-four, Gaspar married María de Atocha y Guzmán. She was the daughter of Luis Ponce de León, who had been Felipe IV's ambassador to Rome, viceroy of Navarre, and governor and captain general of Milan, and Mencia de Guzmán y Pimentel, the fourth Condesa de Villaverde. Ironically, Gaspar's new father-in-law was the great-uncle of his second wife, Gelvira. The marriage lasted but a brief seven years. Doña María, after bearing and losing a son in 1681, died following the birth of her daughter, Josefa María, who lived until 1685.[70]

After Gaspar's 1679 sojourn to Paris with Gregorio, he returned to reside in Madrid. In 1682, he came into possession of his title, the Conde de Galve, upon the death of his uncle. By October 1686, he had married doña Gelvira, and the two were comfortably settled in the capital. Gaspar's letters to his brother during these years are a steady stream of court gossip, news of friends, and prosaic commentary on the weather.[71]

Nothing in the years before 1688 revealed any particular aptitude on Gaspar's part that would have qualified him for appointment to the Viceroyalty of New Spain. Although viceroyalties and ambassadorships were traditionally reserved for the aristocracy, Gaspar's lack of military or diplomatic experience, to say nothing of his youth, could not have made him the choicest candidate. There is, further, no record of his attempting to purchase the office, as sometimes happened in the later years of the seventeenth century.[72]

Possible illumination on this point comes from doña Gelvira's own pen. After learning that she and Gaspar would be embarking for the Indies, she plaintively speculated whether Gregorio might have been responsible for her husband's posting, which to her was clearly a surprise. Gregorio was certainly in a position to influence, if not effect, the appointment. If he did, the question then becomes one of motive and remains ultimately unanswered.

Gregorio and Gaspar, as attested by their correspondence, maintained a close friendship from youth to maturity. Nothing would have been more natural than a loving elder brother taking a hand in furthering a younger's career. Could he not also, however, have finally found an honorable and culturally acceptable way to terminate a relationship with his sister-in-law that was becoming an embarrassment? How better to discourage an importuning and lovesick Gelvira than by putting the expanse of the Atlantic Ocean between them?

The truth of the matter, such as it is, has only been recorded in doña Gelvira's perception of it, however flawed that may be. Whatever the circumstances might have been, one woman, about to begin a lonely journey to the New World, believed she had been condemned to an exile she never sought, but had done much to bring upon herself.

1. J.H. Elliott, "Foreign Policy and Domestic Crisis: Spain, 1598–1659," in J.H. Elliott, *Spain and Its World, 1500–1700: Selected Essays* (New Haven, 1989):120, 123, 134.

2. J.H. Elliott, *Imperial Spain: 1469–1716* (New York, 1966):229. J.H. Elliott, "Poder y propaganda en la España de Felipe IV," in María Carmen Iglesias, Carlos Moya, and Luis Rodríguez Zúñiga, eds., *Homenaje a José Antonio Maravall* (Madrid, 1985), 2:26. When the struggle was taken up again in 1621, it was allotted 3.5 million ducados. This figure must be set against the total government expenses for that year, which were estimated at more than 8 million ducados, in addition to a yearly deficit of about 4 million ducados; Elliott, *Imperial Spain*, 322. For an extensive treatment of this theater of war, see Geoffrey Parker, *The Army of Flanders and the Spanish Road, 1567–1659: The Logistics of Spanish Victory and Defeat in the Low Countries' Wars* (Cambridge, 1972).

3. R.A. Stradling, *Europe and the Decline of Spain: A Study of the Spanish System, 1580–1720* (London, 1981):119–22, 149. G. Livet, "International Relations and the Role of France, 1648–60," in J.P. Cooper, ed., *The Decline of Spain and the Thirty Years War, 1609–48/59* (Cambridge, 1970), 4:414–15. Discussions of the earlier Italian revolts may be found in Peter Burke, "The Virgin of the Carmine and the Revolt of Masaniello," *Past and Present,* no. 99 (May 1983):3–21; J.H. Elliott, "Revolts in the Spanish Monarchy," in Robert Forster and Jack P. Greene, eds., *Preconditions of Revolution in Early Modern Europe* (Baltimore, 1970):109–30; and H.G. Koenigsberger, "The Revolt of Palermo in 1647," *The Cambridge Historical Journal,* 8:3 (1946):129–44. Far less historiographical attention has been devoted to the later revolt.

4. Brief discussions of France's European role may be found in G. Livet, "International Relations," and R. Mousnier, "French Institutions and Society, 1610–61," in Cooper, ed., *The Decline of Spain,* 4:474–502, and J. Lough, "France Under Louis XIV," in F.L. Carsten, ed., *The Ascendency of France, 1648–88* (Cambridge, 1961), 5:222–47.

5. The classic study of the Catalonian struggle is J.H. Elliott, *The Revolt of the Catalans: A Study in the Decline of Spain, 1598–1640* (Cambridge, 1963). For a discussion of Spanish-Portuguese relations at this time, see Elliott, *Imperial Spain,* 342–44; António Henrique R. de Oliveira Marques, *History of Portugal* (New York, 1972), 1:306–33; and H.V. Livermore, *A Short History of Portugal,* (Edinburgh, 1973):95–104.

6. The historiography in English for the reign of Carlos II remains

thin, although efforts are being made to remedy this. For the best to date, see Henry Kamen, *Spain in the Later Seventeenth Century, 1665–1700* (London, 1980). R. Trevor Davies, *Spain in Decline, 1621–1700* (London, 1957):109–63, also discusses this period.

7. Kamen, *Spain,* 22–29. Stradling, *Europe*, 157, 186, 193. Valentín Vázquez de Prada, *Los siglos xvi y xvii* (Madrid, 1978):181, 182. Antonio Domínguez Ortiz, *Las clases privilegiadas en la España del Antiguo Régimen* (Madrid, 1975):143–44, 161. Francisco Tomás y Valiente discusses the seventeenth-century institution of the valimiento in *Los validos en la monarquía española del siglo xvii: Estudio institucional* (Madrid, 1982). Antonio Domínguez Ortiz, "Los gastos de corte en la España del siglo xvii," in J. Maluquer de Motes, ed., *Homenaje a Jaime Vicens Vives* (Barcelona, 1967), 2:115. Carmen Sanz Ayán, "Poderosos y privilegiados," in José N. Alcalá-Zamora, ed., *La vida cotidiana en la España de Velázquez* (Madrid, 1989):154.

8. John Lynch, *Spain under the Habsburgs* (New York, 1984), 2:34–36.

9. Vázquez de Prada, *Siglos*, 320–21, 724. Antonio Domínguez Ortiz, *El antiguo régimen: Los Reyes Católicos y los Austria* (Madrid, 1973):352.

10. Domínguez Ortiz, *El antiguo régimen,* 352, 398. Vázquez de Prada, *Siglos*, 700, 722. Jaime Vicens Vives, *An Economic History of Spain* (Princeton, 1969):444–50, 453. In the sixteenth century, the government also declared bankruptcy in 1575 and 1596; in the following century in 1607, 1627, 1647, 1653, and 1680; Elliott, *Imperial Spain: 1469–1716*, 197, 259–60, 283, 287, 329, 352, 361.

11. Domínguez Ortiz, *El antiguo régimen,* 347. Kamen, *Spain,* 92–95. Vázquez de Prada, *Siglos,* 320, 322. Antonio Domínguez Ortiz, "La crisis en Castilla en 1677–1687," in Juan Hernández Andreu, ed., *Historia económica de España* (Madrid, 1978):36–40.

12. The Moriscos, what remained of Spain's Islamic population after the 1492 reconquest, constituted about 4 percent of the country's total population and 25 percent of Valencia's. Lynch, *Spain,* 44–55. Domínguez Ortiz, *El antiguo régimen,* 348. J.H. Elliott, "The Spanish Peninsula 1598–1648," in Cooper, ed., *The Decline of Spain,* 4:454–55.

13. Vázquez de Prada, *Siglos,* 320. Domínguez Ortiz, *El antiguo régimen,* 348–49.

14. The only exception the crown made to this immobilization of property was to ensure against the concentration of mayorazgos in a few houses. Vázquez de Prada, *Siglos,* 132–33.

15. Vázquez de Prada, *Siglos,* 179, 181–82.

16. Domínguez Ortiz, "Las clases," 123, 149, 151; and "Los gastos," 2:114–22.

17. Vázquez de Prada, *Siglos,* 129, 146, 150–51.

18. Mariló Vigil, *La vida de las mujeres en los siglos xvi y xvii* (Madrid, 1986):11.

19. Aside from León (1527–91), influential moralist writers and

commentators included Juan Luis Vives (1492–1540), Gaspar de Astete (1537–1601), and Juan de Zabaleta (1610–70), among others. Manuel Fernández Alvarez, *La sociedad española en el siglo de oro* (Madrid, 1989), 1:173. Carlos Gómez-Centurión Jiménez, "La familia, la mujer y el niño," in Alcalá-Zamora, ed., *La España de Velázquez,* 177.

20. Women were considered to be doncellas, or girls, from age ten or twelve to age twenty. Vigil, *Vida,* 18. Gómez-Centurión, "La familia," 174. Men usually married at about age twenty-four, women between the ages of twenty and twenty-two. This was four or five years younger than customary for northern Europeans. Gómez-Centurión, "La familia," 172.

21. Gaspar de Astete, *Del govierno de la familia y estado de las viudas y donzellas. Dirigido a doña María de Acuña, Condessa de Buendía* (Burgos, 1597):186–88. Vigil, *Vida,* 20.

22. Vigil, *Vida,* 112–13, 115. Domínguez Ortiz, *Las clases,* 149. Juan Luis Vives advocated instruction in the domestic arts even for queens and princesses; Juan Luis Vives, *La mujer cristiana, De los deberes del marido, Pedagogia pueril* (Madrid, 1944):74. The lot of servants during the seventeenth century was dreadful. They could be retained merely by providing food and a place to sleep and, when serving their masters, did so kneeling all the while. As Zabaleta pointed out, a lapdog had a better place in the home of a powerful woman than did a faithful servant. Juan de Zabaleta, *El día de fiesta por la mañana y por la tarde* (Madrid, 1983):361–62.
23. Astete, *Govierno,* 196.
24. Astete, *Govierno,* 196–99, and *Del govierno de la familia, y estado*

del matrimonio: *Donde se trata, de como se han de aver los casados con sus mugeres, y los padres con sus hijos, y los señores con sus criados. Dirigido a don Martín Manrique de Padilla y Acuña, adelantado mayor de Castilla, Conde de Sancta Gadea, y capitan general de las galeras y armada de España* (Valladolid, 1598):131.

25. Vigil, *Vida,* 49–50, 57. Gómez-Centurión, "La familia," 177–78.

26. Vigil, *Vida,* 45. Gómez-Centurión, "La familia," 176. During the 1520s, Erasmus was widely available in translation in Spain, and women were some of his most avid readers; Marcel Bataillon, *Erasmo y España: Estudios sobre la historia espiritual del siglo xvi* (Mexico City, 1966):287, 297.

27. Vives, *Mujer,* 81–94. In 1523, Vives served as tutor to Catherine of Aragon's daughter, Mary, and prepared a basic, but detailed, lesson plan for her education. The first of England's Henry VIII's six wives, Catherine (1485–1536) was herself well educated, thanks to the efforts of her mother, Isabel I, and was recognized as a scholarly woman by her contemporaries, Thomas More and Vives. Garret Mattingly, *Catherine of Aragon* (Boston, 1941):9, 179, 186–90. The syllabus for Mary appears in Vives, *Mujer,* 711–32. A counterpoint to the humanistic views of Erasmus and Vives were the decidedly antifeminine opinions of Dr. Juan Huarte de San Juan (c. 1530/35–c. 1590), expressed in his enormously successful *Examen de Ingenios, para las sciencias. Donde se muestra la diferencia de habilidades que hay en los hombres y el género de letras que a cada uno responde en particular* (Baeza: Juan Bautista de Montoya, 1575); Antonio Palau y Dulcet, *Manuel del librero hispanoamericano: Bibliografía general española e hispanoamericana desde la invención de*

la imprenta hasta nuestros tiempos con el valor comercial de los impresos descritos (Barcelona, 1948–), 6:657. In light of the then scientific theory of humors, women were characterized as wet and cold, while men were dry and warm. Heat and dryness were thought to increase and perfect rationality. See Juan Huarte de San Juan, *Examen de ingenios: The Examination of mens wits. In which, by discovering the varietie of natures, is shewed for what profession each one is apt, and how far he shall profit therein* (London, 1594):51–68, 278–99, and especially Richard L. Kagan, *Lucrecia's Dream: Politics and Prophecy in Sixteenth-Century Spain* (Berkeley, 1990):36, 62.

28. Fr. Luis de León, *La perfecta casada* (Madrid, 1917):21, 54, 56–57, 182, 190–93.

29. Astete, *Estado del matrimonio*, 125, and *Govierno*, 149, 164–65.

30. Astete, *Govierno*, 168.

31. Astete, *Govierno*, 170–71, 189. Vigil, *Vida*, 55–56.

32. It should be noted that the intellectual formation of seventeenth-century Spaniards in general, even that of the elite, was very limited. Although there are few hard data, literacy rates may have ranged from a low of 10 percent to a high of 20 percent. Gómez-Centurión, "La familia," 178. D.W. Cruickshank, "'Literature' and the Book Trade in Golden-Age Spain," *The Modern Language Review* 73:4 (Oct. 1978):811–12.

33. Astete, *Govierno*, 173–74.
34. Vives, *Mujer*, 102–103. Vigil, *Vida*, 47. Vives also indicated that

Erasmus's writings might be usefully read. Erasmus was placed on the *Index librorum prohibitorum* of forbidden books in Spain in 1551.

35. Astete, *Govierno,* 182.

36. Astete, *Govierno,* 174–75. Zabaleta also shared this metaphor, *Día*, 385.

37. Astete, *Govierno*, 176–79. Vives, *Mujer,* 95–98.

38. Astete, *Govierno*, 184–86.

39. Astete, *Govierno*, 179–80. Zabaleta, while less hysterical, still felt it would be best if everyone read only lives of the saints; Zabaleta, *Día*, 387.

40. The popularity of chivalresque and courtly-love literature, mainly a sixteenth-century genre, continued well into the seventeenth century. Also widely read, and thoroughly condemned, were theatrical works. Vigil, *Vida*, 52, 63–64. Zabaleta, *Día*, 386–87.

41. León, *La perfecta casada,* 22. Astete, *Govierno*, 188, and *Estado del matrimonio,* 84–85. Richard L. Kagan's *Lucrecia's Dream* offers interesting insights into how male domination could shape women's behavior in a religious setting. In regard to the matter of the apple, of interest is the constant emphasis, especially in Astete, on the importance of women fasting. He points to fasting as a positive virtue women should pursue, denying themselves food until

becoming thin and pale. He offhandedly makes the connection between fasting to atone for Eve's original sin by noting: "Be given to fasting and remember how the ancient serpent deceived the first woman with the apple, and God threw her out of paradise with that curse, that she would bear her children in pain"; Astete, *Govierno*, 151–52, 175, 245.

42. Vigil, *Vida*, 62, 64–67.

43. Vigil, *Vida,* 75. Vázquez de Prada, *Historia,* 151. José Deleito y Peñuela, *La mala vida en la España de Felipe IV* (Madrid, 1951):9.

44. Vigil, *Vida*, 71. Deleito y Peñuela, *Mala vida,* 11. The Conde de Galve to the Marqués del Cenete, Madrid, 13 Mar. 1688. Domínguez Ortiz also mentions that the seventeenth-century nobility in general was prone to lawless behavior, and that after the reign of Felipe II, such behavior generally went unpunished. Domínguez Ortiz, *Las clases,* 155–56.

45. Vives, *Vida,* 126–50. León, *La perfecta casada,* 132–37. Astete, *Govierno*, 199–214. The heavy use of cosmetics in part reflected the baroque fascination with artifice. José Deleito y Piñuela, *La mujer, la casa y la moda (en la España del rey poeta)* (Madrid, 1954):192–95. Vigil, *Vida,* 167, 173–75. Lady Fanshawe, a perceptive English observer of the midseventeenth century, noted the predilection of Spanish women, both high- and lowborn, for heavy makeup. John Loftis, ed., *The Memoirs of Anne, Lady Halkett and Ann, Lady Fanshawe* (Oxford, 1979):173.

46. Zabaleta, *Día,* 120–21. Deleito y Piñuela, *La mujer,* 153–54, 161,

179–80, 191–92, 286–87. León, *La perfecta casada*, 171.

47. Deleito y Peñuela, *La mala vida*, 13. Gómez-Centurión, "La familia," 188. A certain amount of illicit sexual relations would certainly be expected in a society where arranged marriages were the norm. In the sixteenth and seventeenth centuries, Spain had an illegitimate birth rate comparable to, and sometimes higher than, other countries of Europe. See Manuel Fernández Alvarez et al., "La demografía de Salamanca en el siglo xvi a través de los fondos parroquiales," in *Homenaje al Dr. D. Juan Reglà Campistol* (Valencia, 1975), 1:345–97, and Claude Larquié, "Etude de démographie madriléne: La paroisse de San Ginés de 1650 a 1700," *Mélanges de la Casa de Velázquez* 2 (1966):225–57.

Although cultural norms opposed illicit sex, there were numerous extant laws that clearly defined both the varying relationships between parents and their illegitimate offspring and the responsibilities of parent to child. See the lengthy discussion in Joaquín Escriche, *Diccionario razonado de legislación y jurisprudencia* (Bogotá, 1977), 2:756–818.

48. Quoted in Vigil, *Vida*, 141–42, from Osuna's 1541 treatise *Norte de los estados en que se da regla de vivir a los mancebos, y a los casados, y a los viudos, y a todos los continentes y se tratan muy por extenso los remedios del desastrado casamiento, enseñando que tal ha de ser la vida del cristiano casado.*

49. León, *La perfecta casada*, 40. Astete, *Estado del matrimonio,* 116. Vigil, *Vida,* 144. The linkage of adultery and honor explains why prohibitions were so strong at all levels of Spanish society; the issue was one of gender, rather than class.

50. Zabaleta, *Día*, 134.

51. Zabaleta, *Día*, 133.

52. Zabaleta, *Día*, 134–35.

53. Vigil, *Vida*, 142.

54. See "Titol de los adulterios é de los fornicios," laws IV and V, in Jaime Uyá, ed., *Fuero juzgo o libro de los jueces* (Barcelona, 1968), 1:176–77. Vigil, *Vida,* 140.

55. J.H. Elliott, *The Count-Duke of Olivares: The Statesman in an Age of Decline* (New Haven, 1986):142, 215, 236, 328, 557. Jonathan Brown and J.H. Elliott, *A Palace for a King: The Buen Retiro and the Court of Philip IV* (New Haven, 1980):172–73, 184–90. James O. Crosby, *En torno a la poesía de Quevedo* (Madrid, 1967):33–35. Olivares's vendetta was finally undone. Six months after Toledo's death, the Council of Castile set aside the sentence and returned all honors and revenues to the family. Juan Bautista Maino's painting depicting Toledo at the restoration of Bahia, *Recapture of Bahia*, hangs in the Prado.

56. Luis Vilar y Pascual, *Diccionario histórico, genealógico y heráldico de las familias ilustres de la monarquía española* (Madrid, 1859–66), 8:410.

57. Francisco Fernández de Béthencourt, *Historia genealógica y heráldica de la monarquía española, casa real y grandes de España*

(Madrid, 1907), 7:126–30. Gómez-Centurión, "La familia," 187. Vilar y Pascual, *Diccionario histórico,* 8:410–11. Infant mortality was 75 to 80 percent for those surviving the first year, 60 percent for those reaching age ten, and 50 percent for those surviving until fifteen.

Ironically, Gelvira's sister also later became the Condesa de Galve when she married Galve's nephew, who inherited his title.

58. Luis de Salazar y Castro, *Historia genealógica de la casa de Silva* (Madrid, 1685), 2:628. Cristina Arteaga y Falguera, *La casa del Infantado, cabeza de los Mendoza* (Madrid, 1944), 2:96–97.

59. Arteaga y Falguera, *Casa del Infantado*, 2: 95, 98, 100, 101, 103.

60. Arteaga y Falguera, *Casa del Infantado*, 2:101, 102, 103.

61. Arteaga y Falguera, *Casa del Infantado*, 2:93. Jerónimo de Barrionuevo, *Avisos* (Madrid, 1969): Madrid letters of 6 Nov. 1655, 5 May 1657, 31 Jan. 1657, 4 Apr. 1657, 7 Nov. 1657, 20 Dec. 1657.

62. Arteaga y Falguera, *Casa del Infantado*, 2:88, 96–97.

63. Arteaga y Falguera, *Casa del Infantado,* 2:126, 127. Salazar y Castro, *Historia genealógica*, 2:623–24.

64. Arteaga y Falguera, *Casa del Infantado*, 2:129. Salazar y Castro, *Historia genealógica*, 2:618–19.

65. Salazar y Castro, *Historia genealógica*, 2:619–20. Arteaga y Falguera, *Casa del Infantado*, 2:131–34.

66. Arteaga y Falguera, *Casa del Infantado*, 2:120, 137, 140, 144.

67. Gaspar's lengthy, affectionate correspondence with Gregorio, which followed him as he traveled with the court, is in the Sección Osuna of the Archivo Histórico Nacional.

68. Salazar y Castro, *Historia genealógica,* 2:629. The Duque de Lerma, Francisco de Sandoval y Rojas, was for twenty years the favorite of Felipe III (1578–1621).

The tercias reales represented the two-ninths of the ecclesiastical tithe paid to the state.

69. Salazar y Castro, *Historia genealógica*, 2:629.

70. Salazar y Castro, *Historia genealógica*, 2:629, 631, 632.

71. Salazar y Castro, *Historia genealógica*, 2:629. The Conde de Galve to the Marqués del Cenete, Madrid, 27 Oct. 1686, AHN Osuna, Cartas.

72. Octavio Paz, following the argument Gabriel Maura y Gamazo, duque de Maura, presents in *Vida y reinado de Carlos II* (Madrid, 1954), attributes Galve's appointment to the court intrigue that eventually resulted in the fall of the Duque de Medinaceli. Octavio Paz, *Sor Juana, or, The Traps of Faith* (Cambridge, Mass., 1988):268.

French merchant Raimundo de Lantéry discusses the Conde de Cañete's purchase of the Viceroyalty of Peru in 1696. See Alvaro Picardo y Gómez, ed., *Memorias de Raimundo de Lantéry, mercader de Indias en Cádiz: 1673–1700* (Cadiz, 1949):301, 305–13.

1. The Condesa de Galve to the Marqués del Cenete, Madrid, N.D., ALS.

Love of my life and my heart,

It is impossible to express to you my great pleasure on receiving and seeing the words written in your hand. In my desolation, this alone could comfort me. Until I see you again, I shall have no consolation. With the passage of time, I am not consoled; rather my loneliness increases. Only the thought of you being so happy gives me some relief. Were it not for this, I would die.

Thus, what I ask you is that you remember nothing that weighs upon you, but only what is pleasing to you. My sister-in-law,[1] in what she is enjoying, has been very fortunate, and I, so very unlucky.

Love of my life, I think it was my uncle[2] who wrote me, saying that he was sending to Guadarrama.[3] With that, I did not want to bother you by giving myself the brief respite I get when I write you, because I have no other. I assure you I expect no consolation until I see you again.

It seems to me I have not seen you for a hundred years. I did not believe I loved you as much as I do.[4] I do not wish to be more bother to you in this life than I have been.

Full love of my life, do not stop ordering me everything you may wish from there. I assure you only this-seeing that you remember me-will alleviate my pain. For my greater martyrdom, I am convinced you will not. You already know with what pleasure and punctuality I shall obey you.

I do not have to make more of what you already know. Because of my misfortune, you will have probably already forgotten. With your glories, it would not be much for you to have forgotten things of so little value. That alone would pierce my soul.

Please forgive this nonsense. I am only carried along by my affection and feelings. I already see they do not honor us, but you will forgive this and other things.

My husband[5] has told me he does not write you, so as not to burden you. He will write to you in Valladolid; I shall, too.

In the meantime, may God grant you a very good journey, as is my only wish. I would be very pleased to see your letters. An embrace to all the ladies of your household. Mine place themselves at your feet.

She who loves you more than her own life and wishes to see you,

Gelvira [rubrica]

1. María de Haro y Guzmán, ninth Duquesa del Infantado. Arteaga y Falguera, *Casa del Infantado,* 2:127–28.

2. This uncle is probably her maternal uncle, Francisco Fernández de Córdoba, eighth Duque de Sessa. She had another maternal uncle, Diego Fernández de Córdoba, first Marqués de Santillán, Conde de Villaumbrosa. Her two paternal uncles were her father's two illegitimate brothers: Pedro de Toledo, abbot of Alcalá and comendador of Lopera, and Fadrique de Toledo, governor of Oran and general of the galleys of Sardinia. Archivo biográfico de España, Portugal e Iberoamérica, fiche 949, frames 409–10. Fernández de Béthencourt, *Monarquía,* 4:128.

3. Guadarrama, a small community 48 k north of Madrid, near El Escorial, was noted for its medicinal mineral baths. EUI.

4. In her expressions of love, Gelvira consistently chooses the verb *querer,* as opposed to *amar.* This reflects a tendency to avoid the connotations of *amores,* which at this time referred to sexual lust. *Diccionario de Autoridades,* 1:273. Patricia Seed, *To Love, Honor, and Obey in Colonial Mexico: Conflicts over Marriage Choice, 1574–1821* (Stanford, 1988):50–51.

5. Gelvira always refers to her husband, Gaspar, as *mi primo,* or my cousin. They were cousins, as were almost all of the members of the tightly knit, closely intermarried elite. Among spouses of their class, the terms *mi marido,* or my husband, and *mi mujer,* or my wife, were avoided. Zabaleta, *Día,* 360.

2. The Condesa de Galve to the Marqués del Cenete, Madrid, 2 January 1688, AL.

Love of my life and my heart,

Even though by this post I did not receive your letter, that does not excuse me from telling you in this one how pleased I shall be if you are well, and your not having written is for no other reason but your laziness. I am ready to serve you; I esteem you again because of how rich you have made me. You already know that it was enough for me to be yours, without sharing your motives, love of my life.

Mateo told me that he had told don Pedro de Castro that you said that of the 10,000 reals he was to be given from the encomienda,[1] he was to give him 6,000 and me 4,000. He says that it is necessary for you to send him some drafts so that he can give a receipt and that he has already written you. Love of my life, in this matter, see what you want to do. Do not leave me idle in your service.

I kiss my sister-in-law's hands. May God keep you both for me. Madrid, 2 January 1688.

She who loves you more than her own life and wishes to see you

Valiant efforts are being made for Luis[2] to marry
the current Marquesa del Carpio.[3] In another
post, I shall write you when I have more time.

1. In the marriage contract of 10 May 1665 between Gregorio and María de Haro y Guzmán, he pledged to his betrothed the income he would receive as comendador from the Encomienda Mayor of Castile of the Order of Santiago. He came into effective possession of this for a twenty-year period on 12 November 1672. The encomienda was worth 10,000 ducados a year, as compared with other of the Order's encomiendas yielding between 1,000 and 2,000 ducados annually. Vázquez de Prada, *Siglos*, 165. Salazar y Castro, *Historia genealógica,* 2:621–22.

2. Luis de Toledo, the third son of Fadrique de Toledo and Manuela de Córdova y Cardona, was comendador of Bezmar y Alvanches. Archivo biográfico de España, Portugal e Iberoamérica, fiche 949, frame 410.

3. Catalina de Haro Guzmán y Enríquez was eighth Marquesa del Carpio. García Carraffa, *Diccionario heráldico*, 84:216.

3. The Condesa de Galve to the Marqués del Cenete, Madrid, 10 January 1688, ALS.

Love of my life,

I assure you that you have me very worried to see the delay in your letters. I have not had one for two posts. Until I have this pleasure, you can imagine the state I shall be in. God willing, I shall receive this kindness. I implore you not to stop writing me, though it may be no more than two lines, telling me that you and my sister-in-law are well. Give me the pleasure of telling me whether it is true that she is pregnant, as some have told me they know with certainty. I have not heard this, because you have told me nothing. I would not think I would have to ask. You already know I am discreet. Therefore, do not fail to advise me if it is true. Until I know, I am furious with you. If you have made of me a thing of beauty, I would wish the same.

My love, I wish to tell you in detail that my father[1] is very proud that my brother Luis is going to marry the Carpio girl. He has made various arrangements. I have told him countless things about everyone, because I see he is in a hurry. I feel very favored that he communicates everything to us, and we do not know what may come of it.

Thus, my husband and I are both very alarmed at sharing these confidences without deserving them. In the end, this matter is in the hands of the Conde de Melgar.[2] I shall continue to advise you of what may be happening, but I do not know that I can tell you of the result. The Conde is half crazy, and the Marquesa's mother,[3] changeable, as you know.

May God keep him and protect you for me more than He does me. Madrid, 10 January 1688.

Do not let on that you know to anyone from here.

She who esteems you more than her own life and wishes to see you,

Gelvira [rubrica]

1. Fadrique de Toledo succeeded his uncle, García de Toledo, as seventh Marqués de Villafranca, second Marqués de Villanueva de Valdueza, third Duque de Fernandina, príncipe de Montalván, Señor of Cabrera y Ribera, and grande de España. He was a trece of the Order of Santiago and comendador of the order's encomienda Valde-Ricote. He was a knight in the Order of the Holy Spirit (Italy). He served as geɪtilhombre de cámara for Carlos II and mayordomo mayor of Felipe V. He was captain general of the galleys of Naples and viceroy of Sicily. His last posts were on the Councils of State and War. He died in 1705. While his daughter and son-in-law were in New Spain, Fadrique held the Conde de Galve's general power of attorney. The Conde de Galve to the Marqués de Villafranca, Power of attorney, Madrid, 21 May 1688, AHPM, P. 10.890. Archivo biográfico de España, Portugal e Iberoamérica, fiche 949, frame 410.

2. The Conde de Melgar was Juan Tomás Enríquez de Cabrera, son of Juan Enríquez de Cabrera, the tenth Almirante de Castilla, sixth Duque de Medina de Ríoseco, and Elvira de Toledo, doña Gelvira's paternal aunt. The Conde is not to be confused with the Marqués de Melgar, José María de Silva y Mendoza, Gregorio and Gaspar's younger brother. He was given the title by Carlos II. Arteaga y Falguera, *Casa del Infantado*, 2:117. Gutiérrez Coronel, *Historia genealógica*, 1:254.

3. Antonia María de la Cerda y Enríquez, seventh Marquesa del Carpio, was married to Gaspar Méndez de Haro y Guzmán, fifth Conde-Duque de Olivares. García Carraffa, *Diccionario heráldico*, 24:65. Arteaga y Falguera, *Casa del Infantado,* 2:127.

4. The Condesa de Galve to the Marqués del Cenete, Madrid, 17 [January] 1688, ALS.

Love of my life and my heart,

Though I have not had a letter from you, I cannot keep from placing myself in obedience to you. I wish you a happy new year. I take pleasure that you cannot doubt that in my love I hope you achieve with my sister-in-law what we have so desired. You both must believe that I join in celebrating the new year. With me, you mark another; may they be so many they cannot be counted. Do me the favor of wishing my sister-in-law a happy new year. Try to write me–at length. May Our Lord protect you for me, more than He does me. Madrid, 17 [January] 1688.

She who loves you more than her own life and wishes to see you,

Gelvira [rubrica]

5. The Condesa de Galve to the Marqués del Cenete, Madrid, 31 January 1688, ALS.

Love of my life and my heart,

I do not tire of thanking God that you have relieved me of the fright you have given us by not having your letters for the past four posts, but I was already at ease with yours of the fourteenth. I do not want to make too much of my despair at seeing myself without a letter from you and learning from my aunt, the Condesa de Cabra,[1] that you were ill. Were it possible for me to have gone, I would have willingly done so on foot. Until I know you are totally free of your headache, you can imagine the state I shall be in, always fearing the very cold weather there and worrying about the very hot weather of the summer. I assure you I am always upset that you are there.

What I implore you is that you tell me in detail what you suffer from. Not to do so is to leave me on pins and needles, but I believe you will do me this favor. I shall put it before all those I owe you. I have nothing more to tell you, but that you should remember how much I love you and that I am away. This alone will be enough for you to see me as you do.

If my vanity is bad, it is your fault, my love. You tell me I should not be so grateful, and I do not know if you are saying it ironically. You surely know that I have no one to temper your absence. When I am with you, it would not be too much for me to thank you as if it were for 100,000 ducados, which to my mind it is. I am only exaggerating a little, since you know that, as far as I am concerned, it is up to you. Thus, what I implore you is that you not leave me idle in your service. May Our Lord protect you for me, more than He does me. Madrid, 31 January 1688.

She who loves you more than her own life and wishes to see you,

Gelvira [rubrica]

PS—I cannot help but tell you that the marriage of the daughter of the Marqués del Carpio is already arranged with don Francisco de Toledo,[2] in the opinion of our licenciado. I shall write you more at length about this in the next post.

1. Leonor de Moscoso y Rojas y Córdoba, the eleventh Condesa de Cabra, was married to Gaspar de Haro Guzmán y Avellaneda, first-born of the House of the Condes de Castrillo. After the death of her husband, she married Francisco Fernández de Córdoba. The Condesa died in 1691. Diego Gutiérrez Coronel, *Historia genealógica de la Casa de Mendoza* (Cuenca, 1946), 1:442. Fernández de Béthencourt, *Monarquía,* 7:134.

2. Francisco Alvarez de Toledo, the tenth Duque de Alba, married Catalina de Haro Guzmán y Alba, Enríquez Haro, eighth Marquesa del Carpio. Their daughter, María Teresa de Toledo y Haro, married Manuel de Silva, the tenth Conde de Galve. García Carraffa, *Diccionario heráldico,* 84:216.

6. The Condesa de Galve to the Marqués del Cenete, Madrid, 11 February 1688, ALS.

Love of my life and my heart,

Though I find myself without a letter from you, I cannot help tiring you with these lines, showing how much you humiliate me by not writing. Yet, considering that it may cause you some bother, I do not press you further. That you are well is what I need. Thus, I do not want to weary you more. I kiss my sister-in-law's hands. May Our Lord protect you for me, more than He does me. Madrid, 11 February 1688.

She who loves you more than her own life and wishes to see you,

Gelvira [rubrica]

7. The Condesa de Galve to the Marqués del Cenete, Madrid, 18 February 1688, ALS.

Love of my life and my heart,

I am so pleased you are already so much improved; I have been beside myself. What I ask you is that you take good care of yourself. You already know you are delicate, and any little thing makes you ill. Thus, I ask you to keep whatever you might give me from the place where you are. Tell me whether the place you are is hot or cold. Though I do not think it will be possible until you leave there, in the meantime, give me this consolation. In the absence I suffer of my suitor,[1] I have no other relief but knowing you are well.

Love of my life, trusting in what I owe you, I dare to beg you to do me the pleasure of sending to Portugal to have made some salvers[2] of red clay, which should be thick, and the ones made for those for chocolate and water, with a hole in the middle for the chocolate cup. I said it the other day to a potter, but he did not want to undertake this.

I am tiring you in this way, as you know I must whenever I have the opportunity. I recognize it is a great impertinence, since you favor me as you do, but you never follow through. You will also send me a little of the heaviest possible pottery for drinking[3] or of the style that pleases you.

My love, I already told my husband what you all sent me, and he will reply to you more properly. What he told me was that it did not seem to him that the Conde de Távara[4] would do what you asked him about sending the marriage proofs[5] to the person indicated. What he would do was send them wherever you order, but not to the people indicated by the individual. In this and in everything, he makes a very upright president.

I shall be very pleased if it is in my power to serve you. You know I have the desire to give you pleasure, as you will experience whenever you remember to command me. I kiss my sister-in-law's hands. May Our Lord protect you both, more than He does me. Madrid, 18 February 1688.

She who loves you more than her own life and wishes to see you,

Gelvira [rubrica]

1. The *galán*, translated here as suitor, was a stock character of Golden Age Spanish drama, particularly that of Tirso de Molina, Lope de Vega, and Calderón de la Barca. In many respects, Gelvira invites comparison with the female character who willingly seeks out situations that were potentially harmful to her family's honor. Richard E. Chandler and Kessel Schwartz, *A New History of Spanish Literature* (Baton Rouge, 1961):82–89.

2. A salver is a tray, usually with a raised edge and indentations for holding cups or glasses, for serving food and beverages.

3. Both red and black earthenware pottery were highly regarded by noblewomen at court. Usually referred to as *barros* in Spanish, this pottery is called *púcaro*s in Portuguese. This simple, porous, lightly cured clay pottery was preferred in Spain for storing and serving water or wine, despite it fragility. The aromatic clay used in the pottery provided a pleasing scent and refreshed the air; the porosity kept liquids cool through continuous evaporation.

Beyond its more conventional utilitarian uses, this pottery was prized as the object of a rather common food fetish. That women of the Spanish nobility ate this type of clay pottery is documented in Spanish literature by such writers as Quevedo, Cervantes, and Lope de Vega. The practice was frowned upon by the moralists. Zabaleta, *Día*, 354–55, 259–60. Carolina Michaëlis de Vasconcellos, *Algumas palavras a respeito de púcaros de Portugal* (Lisbon, 1957):10, 45–66.

4. Francisco Fernández de Córdoba, eighth Duque de Sessa, consort of the sixth Condesa de Távara, Ana María Pimentel. He served as president of the Council of the Military Orders. Don Francisco died on 12 September 1688. Gutiérrez Coronel, *Historia genealógica*, 1:307–308.

5. Women who married members of military orders were

required to submit proofs of the purity of their lineage. María Angeles Pérez Castañeda, *Pruebas para contraer matrimonio con caballeros de la Orden de Santiago* (Madrid, 1976):7.

8. The Condesa de Galve to the Marqués del Cenete, Madrid, 6 March 1688, ALS.

Love of my life and my heart,

I will take great pleasure if you are well, and my sister-in-law, whose hands I kiss. My not having written you these days was because I was bled as a result of my illness.[1] Even though I did not bleed much, I did spit a little blood. With this, I did not dare to write since my head was so very feverish that I was like a crazy woman.

Love of my life, I esteem you as I should for how you have regaled me with the beautiful salmon.[2] I have never seen anything as beautiful. I was a little angry that you had forgotten about me, having sent salmon to Madrid. There is nothing I do not owe you.

See if you want anything from here. You know I am yours, though you do not love me. May Our Lord protect you for me, more than He does me. Madrid, 6 March 1688.

She who loves you more than herself and wishes to see you,

Gelvira [rubrica]

1. Doña Gelvira's health was fragile as an adult. She complains about her headaches and fever throughout her correspondence. At this time, women were thought to be peculiarly prone to severe headaches. One standard home remedy involved moistening the head with a mixture of clay and water. In the event that failed, phlebotomy was the indicated therapy for headaches, as it was for so many other ailments of the time. Luis S. Granjel, *La medicina española del siglo xvii* (Salamanca, 1978):217–20. Antonio Hermosilla Molina, *Cien años de medicina sevillana: La regia sociedad de medicina y demás ciencias, de Sevilla, en el siglo xviii* (Seville, 1970):369–75. Fray Agustín Farfán, *Tractado breve de medicina* (Madrid, 1944):124–24v.

2. Salmon has always been a culinary delight, considered scarce relative to other fish. Around the end of February or beginning of March, fresh-water salmon can be taken, especially in Galicia. They are some of the largest in Europe. Although commonly cured or smoked now, in seventeenth-century Spain salmon was eaten poached, fried, or broiled. Alvaro Cunqueiro, *A cociña galega* (Vigo, 1973):90–93.

9. The Condesa de Galve to the Marqués del Cenete, Madrid, 13 March 1688, ALS.

Love of my life and my heart,

In this post, I have received your letter. Since I have not had one for so long, it was a great pleasure and comfort for me, as you can believe. I am pleased to know you are well, as you can imagine, since I am with you two bodies and one soul. Although you may not love me, love of my life, I again esteem how happy you make me by having now taken my soul. Finally, there is nothing in this world I do not owe to you, and it is not just for yourself that you make these gestures with me. You already know that whatever happens, I am more yours than mine or anyone else's.

I thank you for the pottery. There is no letter in which I shall not thank you. You know that in this matter of the pottery, I must weary you greatly because I like it so. I treat you with so much familiarity, although I know it is wrong, remembering that you are my love.

Courtesy does not permit my not having written you in these posts. The reason was having my head such that I did not dare. With the bloodletting I gave myself, I have improved so much that I can say I am well. You could well think that were it not for this reason, there could be no other for the lack of my letter to you, because I have no other comfort in this life but that of writing you and your writing me. Thus, do not tire yourself further with what you wrote to my husband. Should we wish to correspond every week, we should address them to Montiano. I say every week, if not every day and every instant.

Farewell, I do not wish to tire you further. May Our Lord protect you for me, more than He does me. Madrid, 13 March 1688.

She who loves you more than her own life and wishes to see you,

Gelvira [rubrica]

10. The Condesa de Galve to the Marqués del Cenete, Madrid, 20 March 1688, ALS.

Love of my life and my heart,

  Though with this post I find myself without a letter from you, I am not surprised because of the very bad weather. Yet, I do not want to keep from placing myself in obedience to you in this letter, albeit brief, telling you I am well. That would be inexcusable because of all I owe you, even if I only weary you.

  My love, I inform you how Isabel Solano[1] has concerned me so that you may know. Though these are things of little importance, because they are dependents of my house I cannot keep from telling you. She places herself at your feet and those of my sister-in-law, whose hands I kiss. She and you know that I am here with as much good will as always. May Our Lord protect you for me, love of my life, more than He does me. Madrid, 20 March 1688.

  She who loves you more than her own life and wishes to see you,

    Gelvira [rubrica]

1. Isabel Solano was a member of Gelvira's household who did not accompany her to New Spain. See the Condesa de Galve to the Marqués del Cenete, Mexico City, 2 February 1690, below.

11. The Condesa de Galve to the Marqués del Cenete, Madrid, 7 April 1688, ALS.

Love of my life,

Though I have not had a letter from you for a long time, I cannot avoid tiring you with mine, making known to you how pleased I shall be if you are well. I am well but not a little vexed to have to tell you that the king[1] has honored my husband with the most distant position he had to give—the Viceroyalty of Mexico. This cannot but be a cause of such great sorrow for me, as you can imagine, since I can neither leave my husband nor take everything.

It will serve me not at all to be exiled for so many leagues without having the consolation of seeing you and my sister-in-law. Today, I ask you to tell her so for me. It is impossible for me to write her, because of my preoccupations with the impertinences this honor brings with it. Adios, I shall write you more at length in another post. May Our Lord protect you for me more than He does me. Madrid, 7 April 1688.

She who loves you more than her own life and wishes to see you,

Gelvira [rubrica]

My brother and friend,

My wife has already told you the news of my new position.[2] Although I wanted to write you more at length, the difficulties in which I find myself have not permitted me to. In the next post, I shall do so. Place me at my sister-in-law's feet. Adios, may God protect you for me.

Your brother and friend until death,

The Conde de Galve [rubrica]

1. King Carlos II (1665–1700).

2. Don Gaspar de Silva, the future Conde de Galve, began his career in the royal service as a menino to Queen Mariana de Austria (1634–96), who reigned from the time of her marriage to Felipe IV (1605–65) in 1649 until the majority of her son Carlos II in 1677. On Resurrection Sunday 1675, he was given the key of the gentleman of the bedchamber, but without permission to enter.

Upon the death late that year of his father Rodrigo, the eighth Duque del Infantado, the twenty-two-year-old Gaspar inherited a mayorazgo including, among many properties and titles, the alcaidía of the Torres de León and a regiment in the city of Guadalajara. The following year, 1676, he took possession of another mayorazgo that held the alcaidía of the alcázares, fortresses, and bridges of Toledo and the tercias reales of Ampudia.

On 16 June 1677, Gaspar was promoted and given use of the key to the king's bedchamber with right of entry. In 1678, he was invested in the Order of Alcántara and given the future for its encomienda of Ceclavín. The next year, he accompanied his brother Gregorio, who traveled to France as ambassador extraordinary to carry a jewel to María Luisa de Orléans, future queen of Spain. After returning to Madrid, Gaspar dedicated himself to the study of letters, languages, and to performing pious works. In 1682, he took possession of the encomienda of Ceclavín. Salazar y Castro, *Historia genealógica*, 2:628–32. Arteaga y Falguera, *Casa de Silva*, 2:130–31.

12. The Condesa de Galve to the Marqués del Cenete, Madrid, 24 April 1688, AL.

Love of my life,

I assure you that you have me as worried as possible. Having written you, you have not answered, while we have been tossed out, to Mexico. You have not noticed. Thus, I beseech you: Tell me what is the reason? Until I know, I will be anguishing in my imaginings. Because you have not wanted to favor me, I am unable to think.

Thus, I ask you to relieve me of my concern. In the meantime, I shall continue to ask God to protect you for me more than He does me. Madrid, 24 April 1688.

She who loves you more than her own life loves you and wishes to see you

13. THE CONDESA DE GALVE TO THE MARQUÉS DEL CENETE, CADIZ, 4 JULY 1688, ALS.

Love of my life and my heart,

I shall not be able to tell you with what affection I take up my pen to bid you farewell. The feeling it costs me to remember that I am so far away from you is inconceivable. I had the pleasure of your writing me at a time when I could not do so regularly. Thus, I ask that you not stop doing so whenever there may be a way. This will be a great pleasure for me.

I beg you to entrust me to God, my love. We had a very good journey, though I was very disconsolate and still am. I shall not be rid of this feeling until I regain what I lost. I kiss my sister-in-law's hands. May you be even as hers, for our time is fleeting.[1]

My head aches badly. Love of my life, as I do not know whether I shall write you another letter, I only wish to say to you that my old illnesses, the ones you used to enjoy knowing the state of, are the same. Thus, I just want you to think of me with a new doctor, far from Madrid, and how burdened my heart will be with despair. Therefore, in everything I ask you to entrust me

to God. May He protect you for me more than
He does me. Cadiz, 4 July 1688.

She who loves you more than her own life
and wishes to see you,

Gelvira [rubrica]

1. The topos carpe diem was commonly employed by seventeenth-century baroque poets in Spain. Its call for seizing the moment for pleasure without concern for the future reflected the pessimism of imperial decline. Chandler and Schwartz, *A New History of Spanish Literature*, 310–26.

Doña Gelvira In Mexico City

We do not have Gelvira's impressions on the Atlantic crossing, but we do have those of Gaspar, as related in a letter to the Conde de Bornos in March.[1] Their experiences were probably similar to those of the many other Spaniards who made the voyage to the Indies.

The mercury ships carrying the Conde and Condesa de Galve and the seventy-nine members of their household sailed from the port complex at Puerto de Santa María-Cadiz on 11 July 1688 [See Appendix 1]. A number of slow-moving, large-tonnage urcas, long, fairly maneuverable ships with a high poop and quarterdeck, carried more than 2,000 quintals of mercury, an essential ingredient in the processing of silver ore. The ships headed in a southwesterly direction to within sight of the Canary Islands off the west coast of Africa. There they went west and crossed the Atlantic. When they arrived off Puerto Rico, they turned to begin the final leg to Veracruz.

The rigors of the journey became apparent almost immediately after embarking. Those passengers who were not beset by seasickness, as was Gelvira, in the relatively calm waters off Cadiz soon had to confront battering waves in the Golfo de Yeguas and then open ocean. Supplies for important passengers included all types of dried, pickled, salted, sugared, and honeyed comestibles, as well as such staples of the Spanish diet as wine, cheese, rice, chickpeas, garlic, vinegar, and biscuit in place of bread. Stock on the hoof and fish supplemented the larder. Nevertheless, over the length of the trip, drinking water became stale, weevils ruined the biscuit, and imperfect food preservation inevitably led to spoilage.

Some diversion would have been provided by the presence

of Galve's confessor, the Jesuit Father Alonso de Quirós, and his coadjutor, Father Manuel Navarro. Several important religious holidays fell while they were at sea, and they would not have failed to celebrate them: the feast of St. James, patron of Spain, on 25 July; the memorial to St. Ignatius of Loyola, founder of the Jesuit Order, on 31 July; the solemnity of the Assumption, on 15 August; and the Feast of the Birth of Mary, on 8 September.

The squadron from Spain sailed into the waters off Puerto Rico on 17 August. A convoy of five ships under the command of Adm. Nicolás Gregorio accompanied them to that point. Three days later, Admiral Gregorio and his flotilla separated from the main squadron and headed to Cartagena de Indias.

Upon arriving at the Paraje de la Sonda, they were becalmed. According to Gaspar, this was the most trying aspect of the long journey. On the night of the twelfth of September, when they were finally at the point of leaving the paraje and arriving at Bajo de Sisal, at around two in the morning, the patache that accompanied the squadron spied two ships passing.

Galve lit a beacon and signaled them with a gun, but there was no response until the *capitana,* or flagship, and *almiranta*–the vice-admiral's ship–were joined. The capitana then signaled them with another shot at which their chief petty officer responded in like manner. When the ships were within shouting distance, those of the squadron asked the unidentified ships who they were, what country they were from, what cargo they carried, and where they had come from. They responded that they had been harvesting timber in Campeche. Satisfied with the answer, the squadron continued its journey.

On 18 September at around five in the afternoon, they happily dropped anchor at the castle of San Juan de Ulúa and disembarked. The Galves stayed in San Juan de Ulúa for three days to rest from the voyage and allow Gaspar to inspect the facilities. From there, they went on to Veracruz, where they remained two weeks while the new viceroy put a number of royal orders into effect.

The Galves and their retinue finally left for Tlaxcala on the second of October. They performed their first public function there, an official entrance into the town. This accorded with the role of women of the nobility in the Spanish empire during the seventeenth century, when they were frequently cast as possessions to be displayed.[2] The wife served to demonstrate and enhance the social position of the husband: she was a sparkling bauble, a glittering jewel to adorn him. The moralists of the day described this situation as being perfectly acceptable to men and enchanting to women. Arriving on the eleventh, the Galves remained three days, during which they thoroughly enjoyed the celebrations prepared for them, and visited the church and convento.

On St. Theresa of Avila's Day, 15 October, the party traveled on to Puebla de los Angeles, arriving the following day; they tarried there twenty days. There were many public celebrations, and private ones as well, such as visits to the numerous churches and conventos in the city. They began the final leg of their journey to the viceregal capital, Mexico City, on 4 November. All along the way, festivities celebrated the arrival of the new viceroy.

As had long been customary, the sitting viceroy, the Conde de Monclova, left Mexico City for Otumba to meet his successor and personally hand over to him the Holy Caduceus, the staff of office.[3] Two days later, on 10 November, the archbishop of Mexico, Francisco Aguiar y Seijas,[4] left the capital for San Cristóbal Ecatepec to welcome the Galves. The Convento de San Francisco in that town traditionally provided lodging for newly disembarked viceroys before their arrival in Mexico City, with the tribunal of the merchant guild covering expenses.

After a visit to the sanctuary of Nuestra Señora de Guadalupe on the outskirts of the city, the Galves went on to Chapultepec. There, the *ayuntamiento*, or city council, customarily received new viceroys. After arriving on the eleventh, they remained a week; in the first three days there were three bullfights.

The bullfights the Galves viewed in Mexico City would have borne little resemblance to the modern *fiesta de toros* in Spain and Latin America.[5] During the late seventeenth century, fighting bulls was still considered by many authorities to be an element of horsemanship. Numerous treatises on the art of riding included chapters on fighting bulls from horseback. The most common styles were *con lanza*, or with lance; *con rejón*, or with short spear; and *con espada,* or with sword. Unhorsed bullfighters had to know how to fight on foot as well, though this style of fighting did not become popular until the eighteenth century.

The *torero*'s retinue was not formalized into a *cuadrilla*; rather a number of assistants on foot in the ring performed a function similar to modern rodeo clowns, directing the bull and protecting the rider. Large dogs also were employed to control the bulls. The bullfighter was usually a noble, the aides his servants. In Mexico City, bullfights were staged in plazas that could be easily closed off. Often prominent citizens used the balconies of their homes as stands. The event was a gala celebration, with members of the elite arriving in carriages and wearing their finest attire.

The rest of the week was spent in other forms of celebration. Gelvira and Gaspar secretly went to the viceregal palace in a coach with the Monclovas at five in the afternoon of 18 November, and two days later, he took formal possession of the office of viceroy of New Spain. Because he had a number of matters to administer immediately, he delayed his public entrance into office until early December.

That the event was extraordinary, even given the pomp associated with such activities, was noted by the official chronicler of the university, which participated in welcoming viceroys.[6] The streets of the city were festooned for the occasion, and two triumphal arches were erected, covered with signs, symbols, and poetry. One was located in front of the building housing the Holy Office of the Inquisition on the Plaza de San Gerónimo and the other was placed in front of the houses of the Marqués del Valle, at the door of the cathedral.

In the second week of December, the Galves' first major religio-popular festival in Mexico began with the celebration of the Feast of Jesús Nazareno. A colorful procession left the church of the Santísimo Sacramento to open a new church to Jesús Nazareno. After celebrating vespers at the cathedral, the archbishop and the cabildo went to the old church. Following the solemnities, Gelvira and Gaspar joined the Monclovas in a visit to the house of the Conde de Santiago, Juan Alonso de Velasco.[7] That evening, the capital enjoyed a fireworks display. The next, the leading figures of the court attended the dedication of the new church.

There then began a round of celebrations with different religious orders hosting activities in their respective conventos: on Thursday, the Dominicans; on Friday, the Franciscans; Saturday, the Augustinians; on Sunday, the Carmelites; on Monday, the Mercedarians; and on Tuesday, the Jesuits.

A counterpoint to the nearly continuous religious feasts

was the birthday of the Conde de Monclova on the seventeenth of the month. Two days later, the mood changed again with the dedication of the chapel to Nuestra Señora de Aránzazu, which the Galves attended. On 22 December, the court celebrated the birthday of the queen mother.

Soon after the new year began, the Mexican court was again preparing a gala event. In celebration of Gaspar's thirty-sixth birthday on the eleventh of January 1689, a *comedia*, a regular-verse drama or comedy, was staged. Although the title of the piece performed is unknown, the choice of this particular form of entertainment was a fitting one for the viceroy. When he was in his twenties, the Conde de Galve, then serving as the king's mayordomo, directed rehearsals and acted as assistant director for theatrical productions Fernando de Valenzuela staged at court in Madrid.[8] The repertoire included selections from classic and modern playwrights, including Tirso de Molina, Lope de Vega, and Calderón de la Barca. Works by these favorites were also frequently performed in New Spain.

On 21 January 1689, the *regidor*, or councilman, José Arias died and was buried in the Convento Grande de San Francisco. This was the first state funeral of record during Galve's term of office. In Arias's honor, most of the leading citizens of Mexico City attended the funeral. The presence of the new viceroy and vicereine at such solemn public occasions was one of the most frequent official appearances they were called upon to make.

The following Sunday, a crowd gathered at the palace to sing the praises of Galve and Monclova, who was preparing to leave New Spain to take up the post of viceroy of Peru. On Monday, 24 January, the Feast of the Holy Cross began with bullfights in the plazuela of the Santísima Trinidad. During the second day of bullfights, two Indians died; one was stabbed to death, and the other was killed by a bull. The festivities included the *danza de moros y cristianos.*

The danza de moros y cristianos, or dance of Moors and Christians, in Spain dates from the twelfth century in Aragon. The earliest documented presentation of the dance was at the wedding of Ramón Berenguer IV, the Conde de Cataluña, to Queen Petronila of Aragon in the cathedral of Lérida in 1150. The dance involved feigned battle between Christians and Moors, who by this time had been driven from Aragon as part of the centuries-long Reconquest of the Iberian peninsula from Moorish domination. The costumed dancers' mock combat symbolized the struggle between Christianity and Islam embodied by St. James and Mohammed and was associated with St. James's miraculous apparitions and intervention.[9]

Bernal Díaz del Castillo recorded the first dance in New Spain in 1531. In its heyday, the Moors and Christians was a public celebration of the first order, with all the court in attendance. By Galve's time, the elite preferred more private palace entertainment, such as dances and theater, while for public spectacle, bullfighting grew in popularity. At the same time, the celebration of Corpus Christi lost vigor and was replaced by the feast of the Holy Cross as the most popular festival among the general populace.

Around the middle of April, the Conde and Condesa de Monclova departed from Mexico City en route to Acapulco. The Galves and many of the elite accompanied them as far as La Piedad. On the nineteenth, Gelvira and Gaspar went to visit and bid farewell to the Monclovas in fashionable San Agustín de las Cuevas (modern-day Tlalpan). They traveled to the sound of trumpets with a caravan of six carriages.

Through the spring and summer the Galves set a pattern of semiofficial social activities centered on appearances at popular and religious events. In early May, Gelvira and Gaspar attended another round of bullfights and moros y cristianos in San Pablo, and in two weeks, they were present at the funeral of the wife of Lic. Baron Juan Manuel, a judge of the Audiencia of Mexico. In mid-June, the Conde and Condesa dedicated the chapel of Nuestra Señora de Atocha in the church of Santo Domingo, donating vestments, altar cloths, and a chalice, later paying a visit to the Colegio de Niñas in early July.[10]

A scholarly gathering out of the ordinary run of festivals, funerals, and feasts was held in mid-August to honor Gelvira. A *repetición,* a literary act that was part of the examination required to obtain the academic title of licenciado, was dedicated to her. The candidate was the son of one Diego Franco, and his repetición was well attended.

An important private function took place at the palace on Thursday, 20 October. Gelvira had a birthday party, and a comedia was staged in celebration. *Los empeños de una casa* or *Amor es más laberinto,* written by her close friend, Sor Juana Inés de la Cruz, could well have been on the bill that day, and Gaspar may have had a hand in the direction.[11] Whatever the case, the viceregal palace served as a private theater again somewhat more than two weeks later, when another performance honored the birthday of King Carlos II.

Juana Ramírez de Asbaje, known to the world as Sor Juana Inés de la Cruz, was born in 1651 in the Mexican village of San Miguel de Nepantla.[12] At an early age, her renowned intellect attracted the attention of the viceroy, the Marqués de Mancera, and his wife, the marquesa, Leonor Carreto, who brought Juana to the court in Mexico City to live.[13] There she soon became the celebrated favorite, a young woman of remarkable knowledge, talent, and beauty. During this period, she wrote many outstanding works of both prose and poetry, displaying erudition and complete mastery of form.

The darling of the court was also a driven scholar. Perhaps this apparent contradiction led her to enter the Carmelite convento where she could dedicate herself to her studies. Within three months, however, Juana left the rigorous convento and returned to court. By the age of seventeen, little more than a year later, Juana professed in the convento of San Gerónimo and took the name Sor Juana Inés de la Cruz.

In the cloister, Sor Juana was able to concentrate fully on her studies. Over time, her prodigious literary and scholarly production included poetry in many verse forms, with her sonnets and décimas particularly of note; sacred and profane plays; and treatises on theology, logic, mathematics, and physics. The body of her work earned her the deserved recognition as one of the triumvirate of Latin American literary giants of the colonial period, together with Juan Ruiz de Alarcón y Mendoza (1581?–1639) and the Inca Garcilaso de la Vega (1539–1616) of Peru.

Yet the convento of seventeenth-century New Spain was a much different place than the silent, segregated nunnery of popular conception.[14] Within its walls, the social hierarchy of the secular world was replicated to a large degree. There were wealthy sisters who had relatively luxurious accommodations and private libraries and poor sisters who occupied simple cells. In addition to the nuns themselves were the female servants who lived outside and other, often younger, family members living inside the convento. Most houses had at least one male resident, typically a superior from the male counterpart of the religious order. All was not religious contemplation in the convento. There were lively intramural competitions between groups of nuns, such as the San Juan games where two teams representing San Juan Bautista and San Juan Evangelista tried to best one another in the lavishness of the party they could throw. Social intercourse with the outside world could be fairly extensive, depending on the strictures of a given convento, which varied from order to order. Nuns received both female and male visitors. Among Sor Juana's regular visitors was the Mexican savant, Carlos de Sigüenza y Góngora (1645–1700).[15]

More so than their sisters in Spain, the nuns in Mexico City had direct access to influential individuals in the ecclesiastical and secular hierarchies. They regularly entertained the elite and made clerical vestments in their conventos. On the occasion of several of Gelvira's birthdays, to accompany or acknowledge gifts, and in praise of Gaspar, Sor Juana dedicated some of her finest poetry to the Condesa de Galve [See Appendix 2]. Evidently, Gelvira and Sor Juana developed a close friendship. It was the condesa's custom to visit the conventos from time to time, among them San Gerónimo. At least once, the Hieronymite nun sought recourse to Galve to help return the son of her sister, Josefa.[16] The lad had gone to Spain with some Spaniards, and his mother and aunt wanted him home.

At three in the morning of Sunday, 17 April 1695, Sor Juana succumbed to an epidemic that was ravaging the city outside the convento's walls. Practically the entire court turned out for the funeral service Archbishop Aguiar conducted in the church of San Gerónimo. Unfortunately, Gelvira left no record of her thoughts on the passing of her friend.

The initialization of public works also demanded the

presence of the viceroy and vicereine. On the afternoon of 4 December 1689, they participated in the groundbreaking for the Colegio Seminario to the east side of the cathedral facing the Calle del Reloj and later in the month attended the laying of the cornerstone. The colegio was to serve as a seminary for secular clergy and cost more than 40,000 pesos to build. On the same occasion, Gelvira and Gaspar gave two jewels to the cathedral.[17]

One of the matters Galve had to deal with on his arrival in Mexico City was an alarming report from the governor of New León.[18] Frenchmen had appeared in his jurisdiction–among them, Jean L'Archevêque and Jacques Grollet, who had been with René Robert Cavelier, Sieur de La Salle (1643–87). Galve dispatched Alonso de León on an expedition, which Monclova had suggested earlier, to find La Salle's French colony. The following year, 1690, León ventured into east Texas to found mission San Francisco de Texas. When León returned to Mexico City, he brought with him the children of the Talon family, survivors of the La Salle colony; two more French children came the following year. They all went to the viceregal palace to live. Thus, Gelvira and Gaspar, who produced no offspring of their own, had a houseful of young ones: Pierre, Marie Elizabeth, Marie Madeleine, Jean Baptiste, and Lucien Talon; and Eustache Bréman.[19]

The Conde de Galve's birthday celebration in January 1690 was marked by a *sarao*, a gathering of the court for an evening of music and dancing. A typical sarao, which was also the name given to a particular dance, is intercalated into *Los empeños de una casa,* Sor Juana's comedia.[20] In the play, the sarao of the four nations ends the party. In it, three hundred verses are sung by a cast of characters representing peoples from different lands. Each group, or country, sings the praises of the viceroy and performs a distinctive dance to a particular music until all join together to sing and dance as one.

At the end of the month, the Galves participated in the opening of the Rosario chapel at the church of Santo Domingo. The celebration included one of the most dramatic events in Spanish Catholicism and often associated with Holy Week, a candle-lit procession through darkened streets. At five in the morning, the image of Nuestra Señora del Rosario was carried to the cathedral. She remained there throughout the day until her return in the afternoon. The next day, a Sunday, all the court attended the dedication of the chapel. On Monday, the Conde de Galve's old friend, Fernando de Valenzuela,[21] arrived in Mexico and paid a visit to the palace. He was on his way home to Spain after more than a decade in exile in the Philippines.

One night early in February 1690 provided a new and unsettling experience for Gelvira and Gaspar. Around nine o'clock on the fifth, the Galves experienced their first Mexico City earthquake. It was the first of many tremors that took place during their stay in New Spain. Another quake struck toward the end of the month and another just before Christmas. Still more followed in March 1691 and a final one in December 1692. While they managed to avoid a catastrophic natural disaster, the viceroy and vicereine were certainly veterans of minor seismic disturbances by the time they completed their service in the Indies.

Another natural phenomenon that attracted the attention of the Conde de Galve was the frequent flooding of Mexico City. He took a personal interest in the *desagüe*, or drainage system, designed to alleviate the flooding problem. To assist him, Galve enlisted the services of fray Juan Romero;[22] Jaime Franck,[23] an engineer; and Pedro de la Bastida,[24] a judge of the audiencia.

Between 1691 and 1693, they directed extensive cleaning and repair of the system, utilizing increased funding and labor. Their efforts put the desagüe in proper working order for the first time in many years. Bastida accompanied Gelvira and Gaspar on a tour of the works at the end of August 1690. After leaving the desagüe, they went to the royal mines at Pachuca. Pachuca was a particularly noteworthy mining center in New Spain not only because of the several rich veins located there, but also because the patio process of refining silver ore was developed there. The Galves remained there until early September when they returned to the viceregal palace in Mexico City.

The Feast of the Holy Innocents, which falls three days after Christmas, coincided with the dedication of the *camarín*, or niche behind the altar, in the hermitage of Nuestra Señora de los Remedios. Gelvira was especially devoted to Nuestra Señora de los Remedios. Whatever the specific basis of Gelvira's affinity for that particular virgin, she was behaving quite predictably, at least according to contemporary moralists.[25]

Literally within sight of the viceregal palace, Gelvira had her pick of any number of churches and conventos where she could worship. Nevertheless, she chose to travel to the outskirts of the city, where she often stayed for weeks without Gaspar, who had to attend to affairs of state. The moralists frequently commented on the curious fact that women were always especially devoted to saints and virgins at a considerable distance from their homes and never to the one next door. They explained this as a mere stratagem on the part of a woman to have a socially acceptable excuse to get away from her husband, to travel about town, and to see and be seen.

The church built in honor of the Virgin of Los Remedios

was located near Tacuba on Totoltepec Hill, previously the site of an Aztec shrine. Juan Rodríguez Villafuerte, a companion of Hernán Cortés (who referred to her as Nuestra Señora de la Conquista), had brought the image of Nuestra Señora with him from Spain.

On La Noche Triste, 10 July 1520, Rodríguez secreted her under some maguey as the Spaniards fled the Aztec capital of Tenochtitlan. A local Indian later recovered the image. The Virgin was frequently transported to the cathedral in Mexico City in times of crisis, such as drought and epidemic. For much of the colonial period, Nuestra Señora de los Remedios was venerated almost as highly as Nuestra Señora de Guadalupe.[26] Her feast, celebrated on the first Sunday in September, attracted thousands of pilgrims to the church.

In February 1691, Gelvira and Gaspar traveled to Los Remedios to spend Shrovetide. The Spanish term for these three days preceding Ash Wednesday, *Carnestolendas*, refers to the three days of meat during which Spaniards had parties, visited among friends, and held games for their amusement. Carnestolendas was an abbreviated form of the traditional Roman Catholic festival season before Lent, lasting from Epiphany until Ash Wednesday, characterized by all manner and degree of the pursuit of happiness.

The Galves' good friend, the Conde de Santiago, married María Teresa Vidaurri y Hurtado de Mendoza in Puebla in late April. Soon after the wedding, the couple returned to Mexico City to visit the viceroy and vicereine. At the palace, the conde presented his bride, the new Condesa de Santiago, to the court.[27]

A *mascarada* passed beneath Gelvira's balcony at the viceregal palace later that spring. The mascarada was the quintessential public spectacle in colonial New Spain. It consisted of a parade of people in colorful disguises and regional costumes. Mascaradas could be held by day or night, mounted or on foot. The participants represented included historical, mythological, and religious persons as well as real and fantastic animals. Characters from literature were popular choices as were people from exotic lands, especially the infidel Turk. People from all walks of life and social classes joined in the merriment.[28]

On Thursday, 23 August 1691, at nine in the morning the sky over Mexico City went dark; the sun was in total eclipse. As day became night, the unenlightened masses in the viceregal capital succumbed to panic and sought the comfort of the nearest church. Despite the fact that contemporary intellectuals such as Sigüenza y Góngora studied and wrote about such astronomical phenomena, the general public viewed natural aberrations in the pattern of their lives as omens of evil portent, signaling impending disaster. When drought or flood followed, as they occasionally, inevitably did, the common folk felt their fears well placed.[29]

Gelvira and the family (presumably including the French children) went to Tacuba in late August to worship during the novenas, the nine-day devotions to Nuestra Señora de los Remedios. She carried an offering of a lamp and a complete set of vestments valued at 3,000 pesos. Gelvira returned to Mexico City from Los Remedios in mid-October, arriving just in time to celebrate her birthday in the palace. The present she most fervently wished for, however, would not be given her.

The cathedral bells tolled on 22 November 1691, the day set aside to commemorate the virgin and martyr, Cecilia. They rang out the good news for the citizens of New Spain that the Conde de Galve had been given a cedula extending his term beyond the usual five years. The prolongation of their time was an unwanted, belated birthday gift for Gelvira. Both Galves had persistently expressed their shared wish to return to Spain, and the conde sought no extension. Nevertheless, as loyal servants of the king, they had little recourse beyond complaining to family and friends. It must have been trying to put on the requisite show of gratitude when the archbishop, members of the various tribunals, and the religious orders congratulated Galve on his appointment.

The viceregal couple was further saddened soon after the new year began when they learned of the death of Fernando de Valenzuela. A runaway horse he was trying to control had kicked him in the groin. Gaspar, who was acting as Valenzuela's executor, and Gelvira attended the funeral services two days later. The conde's birthday celebration on the eleventh may not have been as lively as in years past.[30]

Sadly, the series of unfortunate events in their lives was not over. In early February, Gaspar's personal physician, Martín Severino, died suddenly.[31] He was buried the next day in the convento of Santo Domingo. More seriously perhaps, Gelvira's health had taken a turn for the worse.

It has been noted that one of Gelvira's almost constant preoccupations while in Spain was her health. During her years in Mexico, from the fall of 1688 until the summer of 1696, she also suffered from bouts of recurring illness. Although there are lacunae in their correspondence, both she and the Conde de Galve made frequent mention of problems with her health.

Apparently, Gelvira did not experience a recurrence of her illness until some time after her arrival in New Spain. Two letters from the conde, written in the summer of 1689, indicate that the condesa was in good health, though eager to return to Madrid.

Gelvira remarked in her letter of 20 December of that year that she had been well until that time.[32]

By early 1692, however, Galve described her condition as improved. She had been ill of late and had not wanted to write letters. She had also expressed her concern that her letters would not arrive were she to bother to put pen to paper. That summer, around June, Gelvira had a serious onset of illness. Writing at year's end, her husband stated that both of them had been beset by sickness lasting some five months. Curiously, his letter relating their improvement was dated 31 December 1692. That very night—New Year's Eve—Gelvira was stricken again. According to Gaspar, she was recovering ten days later. If that was truly the case, she had a relapse within weeks.[33]

Before the new year was a month old, the condesa wrote that she was very ill and suffering from another bout with her old ailment. She complained the following May of continual illness and another recurrence. By early July, however, the conde could report that she was much improved, if not wholly free of discomfort.[34]

It seems that Gelvira's physical condition did improve for a time. Early the following summer, her husband noted that she was much relieved from the abscess that had been tormenting her and her attacks were not as frequent. She was still uncomfortable with the long treatment but, according to her doctors, not at serious risk from her illness. By late June 1694, however, the condesa despaired that her health was broken; her abscesses had kept her in bed for a month. It was not until another month in bed had passed that her recovery could be said to be under way.[35]

A perilously dry spring in 1692 moved the citizens of Mexico City to seek divine intercession. At dawn on 24 May,

Doña Gelvira in Mexico City

Father Antonio Aunsibay,[36] Gaspar, and Gelvira brought Nuestra Señora de los Remedios by coach to Mexico City from Tacuba. By the beginning of June, it had poured rain three times since her arrival in the capital. This marked the fourteenth time over the years that the Virgin had come from her church to answer the prayers of the faithful.

Easily the most important and outwardly impressive religious celebration on the church calendar in colonial Mexico was Corpus Christi, despite its decline in popularity among the masses in the late seventeenth century. Corpus Christi honors the Eucharist and is celebrated on the Thursday after Trinity Sunday.[37] On Corpus, the church staged a lavish display of its power as expressed through its wealth. Religious authorities in their finest, ornate vestments paraded the symbols and images of the Catholic faith through the streets of the capital. That year, Gelvira watched the procession from her balcony because she was too ill to go out. Three days later, the compelling religious pageantry was swept away by an even stronger force, a popular uprising.

The previous year, 1691, had seen a major failure of the wheat crop in the area around Puebla, just south of Mexico City, which resulted in high prices and short supply. Unrest grew until widespread rioting erupted in the capital.[38] The ostentatious character of the Corpus Christi processions may have sparked the revolt, which was carried out principally by Indians and members of the lower classes in Mexico City and Tlaxcala. A mob enveloped the center of the city, torching many structures, including a number of small shops in and around the Zócalo, or main plaza. The building housing the cabildo was destroyed, as was the granary. The balcony of the Galves' living quarters in the palace was burned; several of the rooms in their private apartment were so severely damaged they could not be used. Fortunately, neither Gelvira nor Gaspar was in the palace when the rioters swept by. Because they were not together at the time of the outbreak, the Condesa and Conde de Galve both had anxious moments as they made their way through the turbulent metropolis to safe haven in the Convento Grande de San Francisco.

The situation was brought under control only after the viceroy mobilized the elite and intervened militarily. One of those who was later recognized for his valuable service was the Conde de Santiago, whom Galve rewarded by naming him maestre de campo general. Because of his ineffective action during the crisis, José de Peralta,[39] who was Gelvira's secretary and alferez of the palace guard, lost his job. Despite seemingly heroic efforts to rally the guard against the insurrection, he was accused of having his troops unprepared, without powder and shot, and of leaving the palace undefended.

If the bread riot of June had been a cause for great consternation, the reconquest of distant New Mexico was a source of joy. That winter, the cathedral bells pealed to announce the long-awaited recovery of the province, which had been lost after the 1680 Revolt of the Pueblo Indians. Diego de Vargas,[40] an acquaintance of Gaspar's who had grown up in the same neighborhood in Madrid, had led the largely ceremonial reconquest. Saturday, 22 November, Galve ordered the cathedral illuminated where the court joined him for a prayer service of thanksgiving.

By the end of the next week, the viceroy and vicereine were again participating in the opening and dedication of a church, the new convento of San Agustín, which opened its doors on the twelfth of December.[41] A procession that Gelvira watched from the house of the Marqués del Valle marked the celebration.[42]

The original San Agustín had been destroyed by fire in 1676; the new convento occupied a large block located a few streets from the Zócalo.

Toward the end of August the following year, exciting personal news arrived from Spain. King Carlos II had bestowed a great honor on Gregorio, now ninth Duque del Infantado. He had been granted membership in the Order of the Toisón de Oro. This was an order of knights founded by Felipe el Bueno (1396–1467) in 1429. The order later passed to the House of Austria, and the king of Spain was its leader. As members of the king's order, knights proudly wore its striking insignia.

On 6 January 1694, the Epiphany, Gelvira and Gaspar received the news they had longed for almost from the time of their arrival in New Spain: they were going home. The king had selected the Conde de Cañete to replace Galve. Their joy must have been short-lived, however, for they learned this was not to be, and more than two years passed before a successor took office. As disillusioned as Gelvira and Gaspar must have been by this news, it cannot have been as devastating as the word that came the following month.[43]

Letters from Spain arrived telling of the death of the Duque del Infantado. We have no record of Gelvira's reaction to this loss beyond her three-line letter of condolence to her nephew. It seems that Gaspar initially refused to believe the news; he waited until he had independent confirmation of his beloved brother's death. Only then did the bereaved Galves, joined by the court, honor Infantado with a service.

Exactly one year and a day after they first learned of Gregorio's death, yet another disaster befell the viceroy and vicereine. While riding his horse in Tacuba on 16 February 1695, no

doubt on a visit to Nuestra Señora de los Remedios, Gaspar was
thrown and trampled. Within two weeks, Gelvira had fallen ill
and been bled for her troubles. She must have recovered, because
in early March she was awaiting Nuestra Señora de los Remedios
at her hermitage. She had been in Mexico City since 24 May 1692
and had traveled from there to Tacuba in Galve's carriage. Gelvira
and Gaspar remained at Los Remedios for a week before returning to the city. On the twenty-fifth, they attended the ceremonial
laying of the cornerstone for the Basilica of Nuestra Señora de
Guadalupe.

That year, a census of the members of the parish of the
Sagrario Metropolitano was conducted [See Appendix 3]. The ini-
tial names on the roll were the Conde and Condesa de Galve. They
were followed by the other ninety members of their household,
which included most of the people who had accompanied the
Galves to New Spain. New to the family were the three little
French boys.[44]

The administration of the household was a task that traditionally fell to the wife, as did the selection of the servants.
Although among the nobility domestic staff was often inherited,
and therefore not chosen by the lady of the house, the events of
that summer must have been embarrassing to Gelvira. A dispute
broke out among Gaspar's pages and some other domestic servants
in his drawing room. Such was the disturbance that some of the
combatants were exiled to Veracruz and others reprimanded.

Although Gelvira must have been struck from the outset
by the rich cultural and racial diversity in New Spain, she never
shared her observations with her correspondents in Spain. Nor did
she evince any interest in the affairs on the northern frontier,
where a number of the most successful ventures of Gaspar's gov-

ernment unfolded. At times, however, the denizens of the wilds came to her doorstep, as when the Jesuit missionary and pioneer Francisco Eusebio Kino brought Indians from the Pimería to the viceregal palace for a visit in January 1696.[45]

Finally, the hoped-for day arrived. On 19 January, Gelvira began her farewells by visiting the nunneries, beginning with the Capuchins.[46] Almost a month later, Gaspar took leave of his caballeros. One last hurdle had to be cleared, however, before he was free to go. In April, the alcalde of the court, Gerónimo Chacón,[47] leveled thirty charges against Galve in his *residencia*, the official review of his term. Legal troubles notwithstanding, the Galves went to say their last goodbyes to Nuestra Señora de Los Remedios as the month drew to a close.

By early May, Galve was cleared of all charges for lack of evidence. Gelvira and Gaspar departed Mexico City on the tenth at three o'clock in the afternoon. The members of the audiencia, the tribunals, and the interim viceroy, Dr. Juan de Ortega Montañés,[48] bishop of Michoacán, accompanied them as far as the Basilica of Nuestra Señora de Guadalupe. Earlier in the day, Gelvira had taken her leave of the archbishop in the church of Santa Teresa.[49]

Prayers were said in Mexico City churches in late summer for the five ships of the Windward Fleet, which was transporting the Galves and those household members returning to Spain and had just sailed from Veracruz. Nevertheless, disaster seemed to stalk the fleet across the Gulf of Mexico. French ships lying in wait for the returning vessels attacked when they were in the Greater Antilles, escaping with a Spanish ship, *El Cristo*. Seventy persons died in the raid, and another two hundred were wounded. Among the missing were the three older Talon boys;[50] Marie Madelaine and Lucien accompanied Gelvira in another vessel.

Doña Gelvira in Mexico City

In those desperate times, the citizens of Mexico City once again turned to Nuestra Señora de los Remedios. On 29 August, at six in the evening, she made her fifteenth entrance to the viceregal capital to watch over the fleet. To the anxious populace, the word from Havana that fall was the answer to their prayers. The fleet had arrived safely; the French had withdrawn in the face of sudden bad weather and illness. The miraculous deliverance of the Spanish ships was attributed to the intercession of Nuestra Señora de los Remedios.

Yet, even that was not enough to return Gelvira and Gaspar to Spain without harm. On 1 March 1697, aboard the capitana of the fleet, *Nuestra Señora de las Mercedes,* some 4 leagues from Cape St. Vincent, the Conde de Galve, prepared a memorial.[51] He added a codicil to the will he had made in Madrid in 1688 before departing for New Spain, which he left in force. He provided for settling a few financial matters and arranging a final resting place. After commending his soul to God, his first request was that his majesty, the king, look after Gelvira so that she might live in the manner in keeping with her service as a loyal vassal.

A witness recorded that, shortly after the ringing of the bells for vespers on 12 March, he observed the lifeless body of don Gaspar de la Cerda Sandoval Silva y Mendoza, the Conde de Galve, in the home of his friend, the Duque de Alburquerque, in Puerto de Santa María.[52] Upon presentation of the original of the late Gaspar's memorial, the Condesa de Galve, thirtieth vicereine of New Spain, signed simply Gelvira de Toledo.[53]

Doña Gelvira in Mexico City

1. Alonso de Losada, was the fourth Conde de Bornos by virtue of his marriage to Angela Ramírez de Haro, Condesa de Bornos. García Carraffa, *Diccionario heráldico*, 77:26. The Conde de Galve to the Conde de Bornos, Mexico City, 25 Mar. 1689, AHN Osuna, Cartas. *The Liturgy of the Hours* (New York, 1975):23–25. The Conde de Galve, Certification of the members of his household, Cadiz, 1 July 1688, AGI, Contratación 5450:47. Mendel Peterson, *Funnel of Gold* (Boston, 1975):69, 70, 74, 83–85. For a description of a similar crossing in 1625 by a new viceroy of New Spain, the Marqués de Serallo, and his wife, see Thomas Gage, *Thomas Gage's Travels in the New World* (Norman, 1958). For a list of the members of the Galve's household making the journey to New Spain see Appendix 2.

The basic chronology of the events in the life of the Condesa de Galve in New Spain follows Antonio de Robles's three volume *Diario de sucesos notables, 1665–1703* (Mexico City, 1972). Unless otherwise indicated, dates in this text are taken from this source. To avoid tedium, we have frequently given only a general reference, such as a month or season. Readers interested in the specific dates of a given event in her life are encouraged to consult Robles's remarkably detailed journal of the daily activities of the viceregal court at Mexico City.

2. Vigil, *Vida*, 119.

3. Melchor Portocarrero y Lasso de la Vega, third Conde de Monclova, was named viceroy of New Spain on 17 April and took possession of the office on 16 November 1686. The condesa was Antonia de Urrea. José Ignacio Rubio Mañé, *El Virreinato* (Mexico City, 1983), 1:155–56, 196 n116, 295.

4. Francisco Aguiar y Seijas assumed office as archbishop of New Spain in 1682. Irving A. Leonard, *Baroque Times in Old Mexico* (Ann Arbor, 1966):199.

5. José María de Cossío, *Los toros: Tratado técnico e histórico* (Madrid, 1947),1:650–52; 2:3–61.

6. Vicente T. Mendoza, *Vida y costumbres de la Universidad de México* (Mexico City, 1951):63–64. Robles, *Diario*, 3:64.

7. The Conde de Santiago died on 12 May 1698. According to Doris M. Ladd, the Conde de Santiago (to whom she assigns the names Juan Altamirano y Villegas, contemporary observers notwithstanding) was born in Puebla in 1669. Doris M. Ladd, *The Mexican Nobility at Independence, 1780–1826* (Austin, 1976):215. Alejandro Villaseñor y Villaseñor, *Los condes de Santiago: Monografía histórica y genealógica* (Mexico City, 1901):52–59.

8. A typical palace production of Calderón's *Siquis y Cupido* on 3 December 1679 resulted in a total cost (wages, sets, food, transportation) of 109,463 reals. In the 1680s, the head of a theater company commonly received around 300 reals for a set piece production. J.E. Varey, "El teatro palaciego y las crisis económicas del siglo xvii," (Madrid, 1985), 3:443, 444. Maura y Gamazo, *Vida y reinado*, 1:200.

9. Arturo Warman Gryj, *La danza de moros y cristianos* (Mexico City, 1972):17–19, 108–11. J. Jesús Rodríguez Aceves, *Danzas de moros y cristianos* (Guadalajara, 1988):11–14, 17–19.

10. The Colegio de Niñas, founded in 1548, provided basic instruction in reading, writing, arithmetic, and traditional women's household skills for poor Spanish girls. There were separate schools for Indians. *Diccionario Porrúa de historia, biografía y geografía de México* (Mexico City, 1964, 1976), 1:462.

11. Sor Juana Inés de la Cruz, *Los empeños de una casa* (Barcelona,

1989):55.

12. Recently, some controversy has arisen about the date of Sor Juana's birth. For a discussion see Giuseppe Bellini, *Sor Juana e i suoi misteri: Studio e testi* (Milan, 1987.):10–14. Georgina Sabat de Rivers, "Sor Juana de la Cruz," in Luis Iñigo Madrigal, coord., *Epoca colonial*, vol. 1 of *Historia de la literatura hispanoamericana* (Madrid, 1982):275–93. A thorough examination of Sor Juana's life and work is available in Paz's *Sor Juana*.

13. Antonio Sebastián Toledo Molina y Salazar, Marqués de Mancera, was named viceroy of New Spain on 30 December 1663 and served from 15 October 1664 until 20 November 1673. Rubio Mañé, *Virreinato*, 1:295.

14. Vigil, *Vida*, 208–61. Electa Arenal and Stacey Schlau, *Untold Sisters: Hispanic Nuns in Their Own Works* (Albuquerque, 1989):339.

15. Carlos de Sigüenza y Góngora was the other intellectual giant of colonial New Spain. Although not the child prodigy that Sor Juana was, Sigüenza y Góngora displayed sufficient early brilliance to be accepted as a novice in the Jesuit Order at age fifteen. After seven years of demanding study in theology and humanistic studies, Carlos was expelled from the order for repeatedly violating its rules by sampling the night life of Puebla. Though he insistently tried to be readmitted for more than a decade, the Jesuit superiors steadfastly denied his requests.

Nevertheless, his scholarly advance continued. Carlos renewed his studies at the university in Mexico City. By the time he was in his early thirties, Singüenza y Góngora was attaining notoriety as a university professor, having won the chair of Mathematics and Astrology in Mexico City. Despite the fact that his university chair included astrology in the title, Carlos championed the application of scientific astronomy over mythological astrology in his numerous publications on various aspects of natural science. In addition to his position at the university, he held a variety of other appointments, such as royal cosmographer, lay priest of the Hospital del Amor de Dios, and official chronicler for the Conde de Galve. In this capacity, he wrote such works as *Trofeo de la justicia española* (1691) about a successful expedition against the French in Santo Domingo and *El Mercurio Volante* (1693), which offers an embellished account of Diego de Vargas's so-called "bloodless" 1692 reconquest of New Mexico. At Galve's insistence, Sigüenza y Góngora undertook a naval voyage, under the command of Andrés de Pez, to explore and map the Pensacola area of the gulf coast of Florida, where they discovered and named the bay Santa María de Galve. Sigüenza y Góngora died on 22 August 1700 after a long and painful illness. Robles, *Diario,* 3:106. Leonard provides a concise, chapter-length review and assessment of the life of Sigüenza y Góngora in *Baroque Times*, 193–214.

16. Julio Jiménez Rueda, *Sor Juana Inés de la Cruz en su época* (Mexico City, 1951):89. For Sor Juana's poems dedicated to Gelvira, see Appendix 1.

17. The cornerstone was laid on 12 December. Eight years passed before the Seminario was completed. Rubio Mañé, *Virreinato,* 1:295.

18. Defense of his vast jurisdiction—stretching from Santo Domingo in the east to the Philippines in the west—challenged Galve. Reports of European rivals, pirates, and rebellious Indians vied for his attention. Fortunately, for a period of five months, the Conde de Galve benefited from the counsel and experience of the outgoing viceroy, the Conde de Monclova, who had been posted to Peru. Beginning in 1687, Monclova had put into effect a series of

measures designed to secure his far-flung jurisdiction. From mutinous Chamorros and English adventurers in Guam to La Salle's Frenchmen in Texas, the viceroy confronted numerous flash points, which, taken together, had ominous potential. His swift responses apparently led Carlos II to name him to the Viceroyalty of Peru after only two years in New Spain.

19. Robert S. Weddle, *Wilderness Manhunt: The Spanish Search for La Salle* (Austin, 1973):249–54. Pierre Margry, *Découverte par mer des bouches du Missisipi et etablissments de Lemoyne D'Iberville sur le Golfe du Mexique, 1694–1703,* vol. 4 of *Découvertes et établissements des français dans l'ouest en dans le sud de l'Amerique septentrionale, 1614–1754: Mémoires et documents originaux* (Paris, 1876–86):43–45. L'Abbé Cyprien Tanguay, *Dictionnaire genealogique des familles canadiennes depuis la fondation de la colonie jusqu'a nos jours* (Quebec, 1871), 1:558.

20. Sor Juana, *Empeños*, 271–81.

21. Fernando de Valenzuela y Enciso was an unlettered, ambitious man who rose to great influence as a *valido*, or favorite, during the regency of Mariana de Austria and, later, the reign of Carlos II. He was born in Naples, where he was baptized on 17 January 1636. Upon the death of his father Fernando de Valenzuela, he returned to Madrid with his mother, Leonor de Enciso, in 1640. There, through the intercession of his grandfather, he came under the protection of the Duque del Infantado, Galve's uncle. He traveled to Sicily on the duque's appointment as viceroy and by 1652 was serving in Palermo as Infantado's page and arms' bearer. Around 1656, Valenzuela had returned to Spain in severe economic straits. A 2,000-escudo gift from his grandmother provided momentary relief, and Valenzuela was able to move in with his mother, now remarried, in Madrid.

Valenzuela's lack of education barred him from entering a profession; he was also disinclined to enter the clergy. He was further cut off from the patronage of the Duque de Pastrana, brother-in-law and successor to his old benefactor Infantado. Through his marriage in 1661 to María Ambrosia de Ucedo, a maid of honor in the palace, however, a new way of advancement opened up for Valenzuela.

Marriage led to Valenzuela's appointment as an equerry to the queen and his informal involvement in Felipe IV's well-known night life. After the death of the king in 1666, Valenzuela, as had the queen's advisor Father Nithard, slowly worked his way into the queen's confidence. Growing trust in him as a valido led to a succession of honors, including knighthood in the Order of Santiago (1671), appointment as chief equerry and superintendent of palace works (1673), a seat on the Council of Italy (1674), the title of Marqués de Villasierra with grandeza (1676), and promotion to prime minister.

Valenzuela's astonishing rise to power at this time was primarily possible because of the debility of the Spanish government. Felipe's death had left Spain entrusted to a junta de gobierno and Mariana as regent until Carlos reached his majority. The junta was a study in mediocrity, while Mariana, so unsuited for a role in government, increasingly fell under Valenzuela's influence. Carlos's accession in 1675 did nothing to ameliorate this situation. Although well-intentioned, Carlos, who also came under Valenzuela's sway, was an ineffectual ruler who by 1676 faced a kingdom in crisis with the aristocracy in strong opposition to Valenzuela's role and don Juan José de Austria seemingly poised to execute a coup d'etat.

In January of 1677, at Carlos's invitation, don Juan entered Madrid at the head of a large force of armed supporters. In conjunction with members of the nobility, he forced Valenzuela's dismissal and subsequent exile to the Philippines for a period of ten years.

Valenzuela languished in exile, having left his wife in Mexico City. When the political winds finally shifted in Spain and seemed to open the way for his return home, he began the long journey back, stopping first in Mexico City to await permission to embark for Cadiz. This provided him with an opportunity to renew acquaintances with the Galves. Robles, *Diario*, 2:236–37. John Lynch, *Spain*, 2:262–67.

22. The Franciscan fray Juan Romero was selected to work on the drainage project because of his knowledge of Nahuatl and architecture. His participation, however, was largely limited to ecclesiastical ministry. Rubio Mañé, *Virreinato*, 4:132, 133, 137.

23. Jaime Franck was a German military engineer in the service of Spain. He began his career in Spain as an infantry captain of German troops in Catalonia. In 1681, he was sent to New Spain where he was largely responsible for the improvements to the harbor fortifications at San Juan de Ulúa. Many of the projects related to the drainage system, which were overseen by Pedro de la Bastida, were drawn up by Franck. He committed suicide in Veracruz on 26 May 1702. Rubio Mañé *Virreinato*, 3:152 n115; 4:129, 137–40.

24. Lic. Pedro de la Bastida served on the Council of the Indies from 16 December 1697 until his death on 24 August 1699. His previous service included terms as judge on the Chancellery of Granada, fiscal for civil matters of the Audiencia of Mexico from

24 July 1681 to 21 December 1686, and judge of the Audiencia of Guadalajara from 6 April 1680 until 24 July 1681. Ernesto Schäfer, *El Consejo Real y Supremo de las Indias: Su historia, organización y labor administrativa hasta la terminación de la Casa de Austria*

(Seville, 1935, 1947), 1:366; 2:458, 464, 496.

25. Vigil, *Vida*, 157.

26. During the war for independence from Spain, the royalists chose her as their patron, while the Mexicans chose Guadalupe. The victory of the latter led to the decline of her cult. Rubén Vargas Ugarte, *Historia del culto de María en Iberoamérica y de sus imágenes y santuarios más celebrados* (Buenos Aires, 1947):209–13. J. Manuel Espinosa, "The Virgin of the Reconquest of New Mexico," *Mid-America: An Historical Review* 18 (Apr. 1936):79–87. Aline Ussel C., *Esculturas de la Virgen María en Nueva España, 1519–1821* (Mexico City, 1975):38.

27. Villaseñor y Villaseñor, *Condes de Santiago*, 54.

28. Leonard devotes an entire chapter to the mascarada in *Baroque Times*, 117–29.

29. Leonard, *Baroque Times*, 17, 193, 204.

30. Valenzuela died on 7 January 1692. Robles, *Diario*, 2:236–37. Genaro García, *Tumultos y rebeliones acaecidos en México*, vol. 10 of *Documentos inéditos o muy raros para la historia de México* (Mexico City, 1981):231–32.

31. Severino died on 8 February 1692. Robles, *Diario*, 2:237.

32. The Conde de Galve to the Marqués del Cenete, Mexico City, 14 July 1689, and 16 July 1689, AHN Osuna, Cartas. Letter 15 below.

33. The Conde de Galve to the Marqués del Cenete, Mexico City, 3 Feb. 1692, AHN Osuna, Cartas. The Conde de Galve to the

Marqués de Távara and the Conde de Villada, Mexico City, 31 Dec. 1692, AHN Osuna, Cartas. Antonio del Corro to the Duque de Pastrana, Mexico City, 10 Jan. 1693, AHN Osuna, Cartas. The Conde de Galve to the Marquesa del Cenete, Mexico City, 12 Jan. 1693, AHN Osuna, Cartas.

34. Letters 19 and 20 below. The Conde de Galve to the Marqués de Távara, Mexico City, 3 June 1693, AHN Osuna, Cartas.

35. The Conde de Galve to the Marqués de Távara, Mexico City, 12 May and 17 June 1694, AHN Osuna, Cartas. The Conde de Galve to the Marqués del Cenete, Mexico City, 24 June 1694, and 3 July 1694, AHN Osuna, Cartas.

36. Lic. Antonio de Aunsibay y Anaya was named Archbishop Seijas's vicar general, or ecclesiastical judge, on 7 February 1692. At the time he was canon of the cathedral of Mexico City. In 1700, he was renamed to the position of vicar general. In November 1701, Aunsibay was named cantor of the cathedral. In 1685, as a prebendary of the cathedral, he held a benefice at Real del Monte. By 1689, he was enjoying a grant of a full prebend as canon. Robles, *Diario*, 2:248. Rubio Mañé, *Virreinato*, 2:48.

37. Trinity is the Sunday after Whitsunday, or Pentecost, which is the seventh Sunday after Easter. Trinity Sunday commemorates the Holy Trinity and Pentecost the descent of the Holy Spirit on the Apostles.

38. Carlos de Sigüenza y Góngora, *Alboroto y motines de México de 8 de junio de 1692* (Mexico City, 1932).

39. Although Peralta was punished, at least one observer thought he should have been rewarded. Antonio de Robles, commenting

on the aftermath of the riot, stated that Peralta had performed his duty as a good soldier, risking his life while others protected themselves. Robles, *Diario*, 2:257. Rubio Mañé, *Virreinato*, 2:51.

40. Diego de Vargas was born in Madrid in 1643. He began his career in New Spain in 1673. In 1688, he was named governor of New Mexico, at that time a province in rebellion in the hands of the native people since 1680. Vargas carried out the first phase of the reconquest of New Mexico in 1692. After the conclusion of his first term in office in 1697, he returned for a second time in 1703. Vargas died in Bernalillo, New Mexico, in 1704. John L. Kessell, Rick Hendricks, Meredith D. Dodge, Larry D. Miller, and Eleanor B. Adams, eds., *Remote Beyond Compare: Letters of don Diego de Vargas to His Family from New Spain and New Mexico, 1675–1706* (Albuquerque, 1989).

41. Lauro E. Rosell, *Iglesias y conventos coloniales de México: Historia de cada uno de los que existen en la Ciudad de México* (Mexico City, 1979):189–95.

42. As a result of the damage to the viceregal palace and other buildings in the center of the city, the Galves were without permanent lodgings for a time. Although they were also burned, the houses of the Marquesado del Valle de Oaxaca, established by the conquistador, Hernán Cortés, were rebuilt. They served as the residence for Gelvira and Gaspar until a new palace was completed. Rubio Mañé, *Virreinato*, 1:157

43. The Conde de Cañete del Pinar, Francisco José de Villavicencio, had promised to pay 300,000 pesos to secure the appointment as viceroy of New Spain, but he did not pay on time. He was officially named to the post on 14 June 1695, but renounced the title. Later he was to be appointed to the Viceroyalty of Peru, for which he made a donation of 250,000

pesos. He died on 20 April 1697 en route from Acapulco to Peru. Guillermo Lohmann Villena, "Notas sobre el Conde de Cañete, virrey del Perú," *Revista de Indias* 3:551-58. Picardo y Gómez, *Memorias*, 301–306. Antonio Dominguez Ortiz, "Un virreinato en venta," *Mercurio Peruano* 49 (En.-Feb. 1965):47 n8. Rubio Mañé, *Virreinato*, 1:158, 296. Robles, *Diario*, 2:299; 3:29, 61.

44. List of members of the Sagrario Metropolitano Parish, Mexico City, 1695, Church of Jesus Christ of Latter-day Saints microfilm collection, 36415. See Appendix 3.

45. Eusebio Francisco Kino was born in the Tyrolean Alps in 1645. As a youth he studied at several Jesuit institutions and eventually entered the order. In 1681, Kino sailed to New Spain, where he was soon in the mission field. He first served in the capacity of missionary and royal cartographer on Adm. Isidro Atondo's expedition to Baja California. Kino is best known for his long service in the Pimería Alta, modern Sonora and Arizona, where he established a successful string of missions from his home base at Nuestra Señora de los Dolores, at Cosari. He died on 15 March 1711. Charles W. Polzer, S.J., *Kino Guide II: His Missions, His Monuments* (Tucson, 1982). For an exhaustive treatment of Kino's life, see Herbert Eugene Bolton, *Rim of Christendom: A Biography of Eusebio Francisco Kino, Pacific Coast Pioneer* (Tucson, 1984).

46. The convento de las Capuchinas Recoletas de San Felipe de Jesús was opened in 1666 and the church dedicated in 1673. The complex occupied some 12,000 square feet and was located in a large block off the modern street Venustiano Carranza in central Mexico City. The church and convento were dedicated to Felipe de Jesús, the first Mexican saint. The Capuchins, so called for their hooded habit, were one of the most conservative of the numerous reform movements in the Franciscan Order in the sixteenth centu-

ry. Capuchins pursued a rigorous, disciplined interpretation of the Rule of St. Francis. The nuns of the convento Gelvira visited were known for their extreme poverty. Rosell, *Iglesias,* 309–12. Lázaro Iriarte de Aspurz, *Franciscan History: The Three Orders of St. Francis of Assisi* (Chicago,1983):195–225.

47. Dr. Gerónimo Chacón was named to fill a vacancy on the Audiencia of Mexico in 1673. By 1688, he was serving as one of the alcaldes of the court. Chacón returned to Spain with the fleet in 1702. Robles, *Diario,* 1:136; 2:160, 227, 235; 3:43, 45, 221.

48. Juan de Ortega Montañés was born in 1627. During his long career he occupied various posts, including inquisitor, bishop, archbishop, and interim viceroy of New Spain. He served in the latter post from 27 February to 18 December 1696 and again from 4 November 1701 to 17 November 1702. Manuel Rivera Cambas, *Los gobernantes de México: Galería de biografías y retratos de los vireyes, emperadores, presidentes y otros gobernantes que ha tenido México, desde Hernando Cortés hasta el C. Benito Juárez* (Mexico City, 1872–73), 1:279–83, 292–300. Rubio Mañé, *Virreinato,* 1:296.

49. Commonly called Santa Teresa de Jesús, this convento was actually San José de Carmelitas Descalzas. Santa Teresa was founded in 1616 and grew to occupy some 12,000 square feet between what are now Avenida República de Guatemala y Lic. Verdad in the heart of Mexico City. Today, the church is usually referred to as Santa Teresa La Antigua to distinguish it from a later Santa Teresa. Rosell, *Iglesias,* 287–91.

50. After being interrogated by French authorities, who found them shy and not fully cooperative, Pierre and Jean Baptiste Talon requested that they be allowed to go to Spain to live with Gelvira. Marie Madelaine was said to be with her as late at January 1698.

Weddle, *Wilderness Manhunt*, 253–54.

51. The Conde de Galve, Memorial, Aboard *Nuestra Señora de las Mercedes* off Cape St. Vincent, 1 Mar. 1697, Archivo Histórico de Protocolos de Madrid (AHPM), P. 12.118.

52. Francisco Fernández de la Cueva Enríquez, the tenth Duque de Alburquerque, was named viceroy of New Spain in 1702, serving until 1710. The Conde de Galve was bound to the House of Alburquerque by a close personal relationship. When Melchor de la Cueva y Enríquez, ninth Duque de Alburquerque, died in 1686, Galve donned a long mourning cloak, not because of family ties, but because it seemed appropriate to him. The Conde de Galve to the Marqués del Cenete, Madrid, 23 Oct. 1686, AHN Osuna, Cartas. Antonio Felipe de Mora, Certification of death, Puerto de Santa María, 12 Mar. 1697, AHPM, P. 12.118.

53. Gelvira de Toledo, Presentation of a memorial, [Madrid], [1697], AHPM, P. 12.118.

14. The Condesa de Galve to the Marqués del Cenete, Mexico City, 7 July 1689, LS.

Most excellent lord,

My brother and lord, lord don Tomás Tello de Guzmán[1] is the nephew of lord don Andrés Tello[2] (may he be in glory) lieutenant governor of the mercury ships that carried us to this kingdom. We received special attention from him throughout our trip. This gentleman is of such admirable qualities that he has known how to win over my husband, who privately suggests that your excellency should see fit to favor him from among your dependencies at that court. With every insistence, I cannot keep from beseeching your excellency to rely on my intercession so that don Tomás may completely fulfill his wish. Because the favor I owe your excellency is already so great, I hope to add this one. This is so that my stepson may know what my importuning your excellency is worth. May God protect your life the many years I wish and are so necessary to me. Mexico, 7 July 1689.

Most excellent lord, I kiss your excellency's hands, your sister-in-law,

Gelvira, the Condesa de Galve

[rubrica]

Most excellent lord duque, the Duque Marqués del Cenete, my lord and brother-in-law

1. At the time of his death in 1697, the Conde de Galve declared that he owed Tomás Tello de Guzmán 13,000 pesos for which there was no documentation. This would seem to indicate a close personal relationship because it is a relatively large loan with only Galve's word as his bond. He instructed his heirs to repay the debt from his estate. The Conde de Galve, Codicil to his will, Aboard *Nuestra Señora de las Mercedes* off Cape St. Vincent, 1 Mar. 1697, AHPM, P. 12.118.

2. Capt. Andrés Tello de Guzmán was the governor of the mercury ships that transported the Galve household to New Spain. Sailing orders, Cadiz, 1 July 1688, AGI, Contratación 5450:47. For a list of the members of the viceroy's retinue see Appendix 2.

15. The Condesa de Galve to The Marqués del Cenete, Mexico City, 20 December 1689, LS.

Most excellent sir,

My brother and lord, your letter of 12 June was of singular esteem for me. In it, your excellency favors me, asking for news of my health, which has been good since I arrived in this kingdom. I have not had a recurrence of the continuous illnesses I suffered in that court. If I am worthy of your excellency's repeated orders to serve you, my pleasure in obeying them will be added to the wish to show my willingness and respect to your excellency, which is my duty. The congratulations you see fit to give me for my new nephew,[1] son of my brother, the Marqués de Távara,[2] was news to me. Very much in accord with my wish, your excellency has my total affection for whatever may be your greatest pleasure. May God protect your excellency, my brother-in-law and lord, as much as He can and I need. Mexico City, 20 December 1689.

Most excellent sir, your excellency's sister-in-law kisses your hand,

Gelvira, the Condesa de Galve

[rubrica]

THE NEW WORLD LETTERS

Most excellent lord duque, the Duque and
Marqués del Cenete, my brother-in-law and lord

1. Either Francisco de Toledo or Miguel de Toledo y Pimentel.

2. The Marqués de Távara, Gelvira's older brother Antonio de Toledo, was the second son of Fadrique de Toledo and Manuela de Córdova y Cardona. He was comendador of Azuaga in the Order of Santiago. He married Ana María de Córdova y Pimentel, the eighth proprietary Marquesa de Távara and Condesa de Villada. Their children were Francisco de Toledo, the Conde de Villada (married Catalina Ventura Colón y Portugal; died without succession) and Miguel de Toledo y Pimentel, who became the Conde de Villada on his brother's death. He in turn married María Francisca Alfonsa de Silva y Mendoza, firstborn child of Juan de Dios de Silva y Mendoza, the Duque del Infantado, Pastrana, and Francavila, and María Teresa de los Ríos. Archivo biográfico de España, Portugal e Iberoamérica, fiche 949, frames 410, 413.

16. The Condesa de Galve to the Marqués del Cenete, Mexico City, 28 January 1690, LS.

Most excellent lord,

My brother in-law and lord, in your letter of 30 June of last year, 1689, your excellency orders me to aid the two religious of the Order of Our Father, San Francisco, who came to this kingdom to collect alms for the canonization of San Pedro Regalados.[1] Given that this is an order from you, beyond being an act of such piety, your excellency may be sure that for my part, I shall do everything I can to see that they are successful as possible in collecting alms. To this end, I shall encourage others to cooperate and assist them with alms, because this so redounds to the service of God. There is also great need among the religious from other orders and churches dedicated to other saints.

These religious have not come to see me as yet. Believe me your excellency, I shall seek out and aid them any way I can. I long to have many opportunities to serve you and make you happy. Then you may know my good will and affection.

May Our Lord protect your most excellent person the many years I need. Mexico City,

28 January 1690.

Most excellent lord, your sister-in-law
and least of your servants kisses your excellency's
hand,

Gelvira, the Condesa de Galve [rubrica]

Most excellent lord duque, Duque Marqués del
Cenete, my brother-in-law and lord

1. San Pedro Regalados (1390–1456), born of a noble family in Valladolid, entered that city's Franciscan convento at the age of thirteen with the reluctant permission of his widowed mother. He joined the strictly Observant convento Peter Villacretios established at Tribulos, where he became known for his austere life and fervent religious practices. He succeeded Villacretios at his death and received the epithet Regalados (Lat. Regalatus) for his rigorous enforcement of the Rule. He was later canonized by Benedict XIV (1740–58). Herbert Thurston and Donald Attwater, eds., *Butler's Lives of the Saints* (New York, 1956), 2:303.

17. The Condesa de Galve to the Marqués del Cenete, Mexico City, 2 February 1690, ALS.

Most excellent lord,

My brother-in-law and lord, your lord-ship is well aware that Isabel Solano served me faithfully and with love until she married in Chamartín.[1] She has now written me that she misses me and tells me of some difficulties. Though her husband is a good man, he has no skill to employ to earn his keep. Since I have loved her well, and wished for relief and the remedy of her difficulties, I cannot keep from beseeching your excellency to see fit to give me the gift of favoring her and her husband. You can accommodate him in something you think suit-able so that he can be the breadwinner. I shall esteem your excellency for having recommended him for whatever occurs to you. I assure your excellency that I love Isabel well, for the special affection with which she served me. I hope that this will be enough so that your excellency will not forget her. Please give me many opportunities to serve your excellency in ways that will make you happy. May God protect your most excellent person the many years I wish.

Mexico, 2 February 1690.

    Most excellent lord, your excellency's sister-in-law and least of your servants
kisses your hands,

    Gelvira, the Condesa de Galve [rubrica]

Most excellent lord duque, the Duque and
Marqués del Cenete, brother-in-law and lord

1. Chamartín de la Rosa, known for its fresh air and healthy climate, was located north-northwest of Madrid, in the outskirts of the city. In 1679, Catalina de Sandoval y Mendoza, the Duquesa del Infantado, purchased the property, which had been previously owned by her then deceased husband, Ruy Gómez de Silva, príncipe de Melito, the fourth Duque de Pastrana. He had created a recreation area there that included beautiful gardens designed by the noted architects Agustín de Pedrosa and Juan de Herrera. On the death of his mother, the eighth Duquesa del Infantado, on 19 July 1686, don Gregorio inherited Charmartín. Arteaga y Falguera, *Casa del Infantado*, 2:136. Madoz, *Diccionario,* 7:297–98.

18. The Condesa de Galve to the Marqués del Cenete, Mexico City, 21 August 1692, LS.

Most excellent lord,

My brother-in-law and lord, by Juan de Montúfar's letter,[1] which he sent by irregular means, that arrived in my husband's hands in May of this year, I received word that his majesty (may God keep him) named you to the Council of State.[2] Because it falls to me to congratulate you, I am availing myself of this means to demonstrate that this news has been the cause for singular rejoicing. I can assure your excellency truthfully that this was necessary to tolerate the uneasiness this land suffers and the solitude with which one lives. To this is added the great sorrow and fright I had on 8 June because of the Indian riot.[3] This disappointment caused me great displeasure, the more so because of the risk to my husband, who must be greatly pitied. His good intentions, zeal, and disinterest in the service of his majesty (may God keep him) were not enough to keep him from experiencing this, nor were the numerous measures he had taken, because he was alone, anticipating what happened.

Now, thanks to Our Lord, the calm continues. Since yesterday, he has been busy with preparations and repairs he has begun. I am at your excellency's disposition. You can order me with the assurance that it will be obeyed. May God keep the excellent person of your excellency, my lord and my brother-in-law, the many years He can. Mexico City, 21 August 1692.

Most excellent lord, your sister-in-law and surest servant kisses your excellency's hands,

Gelvira, the Condesa de Galve [rubrica]

Most excellent lord duque, the Duque and Marqués del Cenete, my lord and brother-in-law

THE NEW WORLD LETTERS

1. Juan de Montúfar was a trusted agent and member of the Conde de Galve's household. While the conde was serving in New Spain, Montúfar administered his incomes and expenses in Spain and exercised his power of attorney for related matters. In the memorial to his will, the conde asked Gelvira to treat don Juan as though he were a member of her household. She was also to see he was given 3,000 vellon ducados, in addition to remuneration for his services, to arrange the marriage of one of his daughters. The Conde de Galve, Memorial, Aboard *Nuestra Señora de las Mercedes,* 1 Mar. 1697. AHPM, P. 12.118. The Conde de Galve to Juan de Montúfar, Transfer, Madrid, 21 May 1688, AHPM, 10.890. The Conde de Galve to Juan de Montúfar, Power of attorney, Madrid, 21 May 1688, AHPM, P. 10.890.

2. Under Carlos I and Felipe II, the Council of State discussed all political and military matters of the crown. During the reign of Carlos II, however, the council was a largely honorary body, and authority to directly advise the king resided in the Secretaries of State and Despacho Universal. Janine Fayard, *Les membres du Conseil de Castille a l'époque moderne, 1621–1746* (Geneva, 1979):136–37, 430 n45.

3. In the late afternoon of 8 June 1692, rioting erupted at the granary in Mexico City. Shortages of wheat and maize, the result of bad weather in late 1691 in the Puebla district, in combination with hoarding had resulted in high prices and great hardship in Mexico City, particularly among the lower classes. The situation was not alleviated by the Conde de Galve's provision of credit in the spring of 1692 to permit purchase of maize at moderate prices at the granary.

By his own admission, Galve was caught unaware by the riots.

The eighth was a feast day, and the viceroy was visiting the Convento of San Francisco. He was joined there by the condesa, who had narrowly escaped the rioters while returning to the palace. Cut off from the palace guard, some of whom were attempting to stem the violence, Galve nevertheless managed to organize the city's leading citizens, under the leadership of the Conde de Santiago, into an effective resistance. By the morning of 9 June, various militia companies of infantry and cavalry were on guard throughout the city, and they had successfully apprehended some of the rioters and confiscated their booty.

In the wake of the disorders, fueled, according to Galve, by the excessive consumption of pulque, property damages could be assessed. Arsonists had caused the greatest destruction. All the gateways into the viceregal palace, which had been closed to prevent the rioters' entry, were burned. Much of the palace was destroyed and had to be rebuilt. The four rooms the viceroy and his family occupied, which faced the plaza, were severely affected. Parts of the prison, the criminal chamber, the audiencia, and the upper room of the armory were also burned. The old section of the cabildo building was lost, as were sections of the granary. Most heavily damaged were the plaza and adjacent shops, which suffered the effects of both fire and looting.

On 14 June, following the example of Mexico City, the Indians of Tlaxcala and other pueblos also rose up, burning the residence of the alcalde mayor. In response to these outbreaks of violence, Galve ordered all Spaniards, mulattoes, and mestizos in Mexico City armed and formed into militia companies, partially at crown expense. He also instituted a ban on the sale of pulque, a drastic step, since sales generated approximately 150,000 pesos for the government each year. The final estimated cost of the damages done during the rioting was 3 million pesos. Andrés Cavo, *Historia de Mexico* (Mexico City, 1949):365. The Conde de Galve to the king, Mexico City, 28 June 1693, AHN, Osuna, Cartas. The Conde de Galve to the king, Mexico City, 30 June 1692, AHN, Sección Osuna. The Conde de Galve to the Marqués del Cenete, Mexico City, 23 Aug. 1692, AHN, Osuna, Cartas. Carlos de Sigüenza y Góngora, *Alboroto y motín.*

19. The Condesa de Galve to the Marqués del Cenete, Mexico City, January 1693, LS.

Most excellent lord,

My brother-in-law and lord, I respond to two letters from your excellency, dated 14 July 1691 and 20 June of last year. The news your excellency sees fit to give me that you continue in perfect health leaves me pleased. I pray to Our Lord that it will be so for many years. I can tell your excellency that my health is very bad. I still suffer from my old ailment, which troubles me mightily. Nevertheless, I hope your excellency will give me many occasions to serve you in ways that will make you happy. May Our Lord protect your excellency many years, as I wish. Mexico, January 1693.

Most excellent lord, your sister-in-law and least servant kisses your excellency's hands,
Gelvira, the Condesa de Galve [rubrica]

Most excellent lord duque, the Duque and Marqués del Cenete, my brother-in-law and lord

20. The Condesa de Galve to the Duquesa del Infantado, Mexico City, 20 January 1693, ALS.

Most excellent lady,

My lady, sister-in-law, and lifelong friend, with the packet boat and fleet that made port in these kingdoms, I have received your three letters, dated 16, 17, and 26 June of last year. The last one left me concerned, as you can imagine, for what you tell me of the tertian fever[1] having recurred. I pray to Our Lord that you have already gotten better, as I affectionately wish for you, and that my brother-in-law and nephews enjoy perfect health.

I assure you I am very worried to see how hard my brother-in-law is working, and no less so by my husband, who places himself at your feet. There is a great deal of work here, and he has suffered much from ill health.[2] Glory be to God, he is much better, which is no small thing given the cares and afflictions he has had. That court was informed of this by the preceding packet boat that left for those kingdoms.

I am very ill, because the ailment I suffered in that court and here has recurred. I had to be bled twice. Although I am better, I am always fearful it will return.

Thank you very much for the gift I received by the hand of Benito from Cartagena[3] Everything is very much as if from your hand. I cannot help telling you that trade with France and England is almost unheard of, but you can do anything.[4] I remain very fond of the gift and esteem it as I should. I was very happy with the news you gave me of my nephews, the Lemos boys,[5] having returned to that court, so that you will have the satisfaction of having them near.

Since you know how much I wish to serve you, do not refrain from ordering me. I shall postpone until the fleet's return writing you more at length. I shall send you what is produced from what came in the mercury ships as you order me. May Our Lord keep you, my lady and sister-in-law, many years in the company of my brother-in-law, whose hands I kiss. Mexico City, 20 January 1693.

My lady and sister-in-law, because of my affection for you, you must believe that I am vexed by your poor health, since only we who experience it know how much trouble it is. I trust in God that you will have completely recovered.[6] This is what I do not know how to do: just when I seem to be getting better, I get worse. May God give me patience for my impatience in not having been able to send you those little nothings. It seems they just cannot seem to get there. I shall be pleased if you are satisfied that I am trying to serve you. They will go in the next fleet, and I shall write you.

Most excellent lady, your sister-in-law and friend kisses your hands,

Gelvira [rubrica]

Most excellent lady, the Duquesa del Infantado, my lady, my sister, and friend

1. Tertian fever is an intermittent fever that recurs every third day. It is often associated with vivax malaria, which is caused by the parasite *Plasmodium vivax*.

2. Galve was in ill health much of the time he served in New Spain. By secret cedula of 27 May 1688, before he even left Spain, he learned that his term of office was to be extended beyond the usual three years stipulated in the *Recopilación de leyes de las Indias*. He requested that he be allowed to return to Spain on several occasions. The king granted permission in 1695, but did not find a successor until the following year. Rubio Mañé, *Virreinato*, 1:158, 200–210. *Recop*. Lib. 3, tít. 3, ley 71. AGI México, 610 contains several documents relating to Galve's appointment and requests for permission to return to Spain.

3. Cartagena (de Indias) in the Viceroyalty of New Granada, on the northwest coast of present-day Colombia, was one of the most important cities in Spanish colonial America. After the galleón, the annual fleet from Spain to the South American continent, put in and unloaded at its port-of-call, Portobello on the Isthmus of Panama, it sailed to heavily fortified Cartagena to await the time for the return voyage.

4. Officially, direct trade between England and France and the Spanish New World colonies was illegal. On the basis of the treaties of Tordesillas, Pope Alexander VI issued a series of bulls beginning in 1492 that divided the known and as yet undiscovered world—not already in the hands of other European nations—between Spain and Portugal. In practice, this demarcation was largely ignored by the other European powers. Between 1625 and 1650 the English, French, and Dutch had settled most of the islands of the Lesser Antilles. The Dutch took Curaçao in 1634, in 1655 the English occupied Jamaica, and by 1665, the French held

the north of the island of Hispaniola. The islands' enclaves became centers of an active contraband trade with the Spanish colonies so some goods of English and French manufacture did enter New Spain. When the fleet system collapsed during the War of the Spanish Succession following the death of Carlos II in 1700, Spain's European rivals regularly supplied the American colonies. C.H. Haring, *The Spanish Empire in America* (1943, rpt.; New York, 1963):7, 79, 310–15.

5. The children of Pedro Antonio Fernández de Castro y Portugal, the tenth Conde de Lemos, and Ana Francisca Hermengilda de Borja y Centellas Doria y Colonna were doña Gelvira's nephews and nieces by marriage. On 8 September 1687, Ginés Francisco Ruiz de Castro y Portugal, their oldest son, married Catalina María Lorenza de Silva y Haro de la Vega y Luna, second daughter of the Duques del Infantado. The other Lemos children were Salvador Francisco Ruiz de Castro y Portugal, who died in August 1694; Francisco Fernández de Castro y Portugal, who fell in battle in the Low Countries in June 1692; María Alberta Antonia Fernández de Castro y Portugal, who lived until 1706; and Rosa Francisca de Castro y Portugal, who died as a child while her father was viceroy of Peru. Fernández de Béthencourt, *Monarquía,* 4:564–74.

6. It seems that the Duquesa del Infantado, María de Haro y Guzmán, suffered from the same malady as Gelvira. María never saw this letter, which left for Spain on the packet boat on 29 January 1693, because she died on 10 February. Arteaga y Falguera, *Casa del Infantado*, 2:141–42. Robles, *Diario,* 2:284.

21. The Condesa de Galve to the Marqués de Távara, Mexico City, 28 May 1693, L and ALS.

My brother and love of my life,

With the occasion of this fleet,[1] which is making its return trip, I have not wanted to miss writing you these lines to tell you through them how pleasing it will be for me to know that you, my sister-in-law, and the rest of my nieces and nephews are in perfect health. May it continue for the many years I wish. I remain ready to serve you, though I cannot overcome my continual aliments. They are not much helped by the vices here.

The nightmares of these past days have been terrible. By now, you will have had news of them by my letter, which I sent in the last packet boat. What I regret now is that our return to those kingdoms is not to be on this occasion. My only consolation is the hope that it will be on the next one. I assure you I desire it greatly. Here there is no way to improve or recover my health.

My husband, glory be to God, is convalescent. He has also suffered a significant decline in his health. I kiss your hands and ask you, well, you know I am very much yours. Do not refrain from ordering me whatever you may wish. May Our Lord protect you, my beloved brother, the many years I wish. Mexico City, 28 May 1693.

My love, there is nothing here to write about, except that these troubles remain calm. What we saw has caused a justified lack of confidence. Given that I have not written anything but lamentations since I came, I shall do no better than usual this time and with better reason. My ailment worsens every day. I assure you I am old and spent, but with hope that by going there I shall recover. My husband is better, though vomiting daily and having dizzy spells[2] that have me very worried. You, who are not suffering, write me at length. This is the only pleasure I can have here. Adios.

Yours beyond death, though you do not want it so,

Gelvira [rubrica]

The Marqués de Távara, my brother and lord

1. The mail was sent to Veracruz on 5 June 1693, but the fleet did not sail for Spain until 15 July. Robles, *Diario*, 2:290, 292.

2. Galve's symptoms clearly indicate the presence of the "intermittent fevers" that were the bane of seventeenth-century medicine. Even a slight attack could produce vomiting, cough, pain in the side affecting breathing, violent headaches, and giddiness. Medical personnel of this time were preoccupied with the clinical problem presented by fevers, such as malaria, that sometimes reached epidemic proportions. The study of malarial fevers was well advanced; by the late sixteenth century, Luis Mercado, physician to both Felipe II and Felipe III, had already described and classified them in his *Opera medica*. While they were fairly easily diagnosed, they were not necessarily effectively treated. Rudimentary herbal medicines probably provided some relief, but the true therapeutic revolution came in the 1630s, when Spaniards learned of Indian use of quinine bark in Peru. Its introduction and slow acceptance in Spain in the 1640s, and its fervent propagation by the Jesuits throughout Europe, did much to aid medical treatments of the time. James Lind, *An Essay on Diseases Incidental to Europeans in Hot Climates, with the Method of Preventing Their Fatal Consequences* (Philadelphia, 1811):224–25. Granjel, *La medicina española*, 174. Carlos Enrique Paz Soldán, *Las tercianas del Conde de Chinchón* (Lima, 1935):47.

22. The Condesa de Galve to the Duquesa del Infantado y Pastrana, Marquesa del Cenete, Mexico City, 28 May 1693, LS.

Most excellent lady,

My lady, sister-in-law, and lifelong friend, in the last packet boat I wrote you and now I do so again because of the great pleasure I take in it and also for the news I wish to have of your health. I shall be happy if it is as good as I wish and if it is the same with my brother-in-law and nephews, whose hands I kiss. My husband places himself at your feet. I remain to serve you in everything, though very ill, because the recurrence of my illness has caused me headaches so severe that I am prevented from writing in my own hand. You will therefore excuse its being written in someone else's hand. Now, I shall go on to tell you that I am sending the money, as you have ordered me, by don Pablo Vizarrón.[1] You can rely on him whenever you want to send something. I am very pleased to have successfully served you, and by what you tell me about my not sending you something that may break.

For this reason, no pottery[2] is coming. I am only sending you an image of Guadalupe,[3] painted from the original, since you are so devoted to the Lady, and some chocolate.[4] I shall be happy if it is to your liking. With that, you will not notice that the fans[5] I am sending you are not very good. Since the boat from China[6] did not come this year, nothing was to be found. You will thus pardon the insignificance of the gift. When I come, I shall try to bring some of the best.

I wish the day had already arrived when we might see one another in that court. In the meantime, do not fail to order me, since you know I am very much yours. May Our Lord protect you, my lady and sister-in-law, the many years I wish. Mexico City, 28 May 1693.

My love, here is the list from the raffles, if it would please you to entertain yourself reading it and so that you will know that I am a businesswoman. The money I asked for is being used for the cacao[7] so that don Pablo Vizarrón can sell it and send you an accounting. Because he is my husband's agent and a very reputable man, I sent it to him, saying that he should do what you order him to. I shall be pleased if you like this arrangement, since that is my wish. I am as always, and there is nothing new here. Everything is quiet.

      Most excellent lady, your sister-in-law and surest friend kisses your hands,

      Gelvira [rubrica]

Most excellent lady duquesa, the Duquesa del Infantado y Pastrana, Marquesa del Cenete, my lady, sister-in-law, and friend

Record of the pieces of crystal sent to be sold with the highest prices at which they could be appraised, which served as a guide for the raffle (although with some variation).

A small worked, cup decorated with red and green enamel, appraised at 80 pesos.
Another cup with a tiny decoration at the tip of its base, appraised at 74 pesos.
A small, smooth crystal shield with a gilt base and handles, appraised at 64 pesos.
A small, worked dicebox without any decora-

tion, appraised at 120 pesos.
Another dicebox with a lid and handles, with some decoration, appraised at 100 pesos.
A goblet from Carmona[8] with base, appraised at 200 pesos.
A water jug with gilt handle and base with some inlaid pearls and rubies, appraised at 100 pesos.

A round flask with gilt, black enamel mouth, appraised at 12 pesos.
Another, more flat-nosed crystal flask, appraised at 10 pesos.
A crystal cask without a lid, appraised at 10 pesos.
Another little crystal cask with a lid to one side, appraised at 10 pesos.
Three small crystal cases without decoration, appraised at 24 pesos each, which comes to 72 pesos.

A round, flat-nosed, decorated crystal box, appraised at 14 pesos.
A long, decorated crystal box, appraised at 12 pesos.
Inside the box, another small worked crystal box with small black enamel metal springs and four turquoises, appraised at 26 pesos.
Another decorated crystal box in the form of a heart, appraised at 16 pesos.

A tiny crystal chestnut, appraised at 12 pesos.

Two small crystal casks with taps, appraised at 20 pesos.

A crystal globe, appraised at 14 pesos.

A blue, decorated crystal box, appraised at 10 pesos.

A crystal, egg-shaped card with merlon-shaped decoration on which a San Antonio is painted, appraised at 40 pesos.

A pair of drop earrings in the form of eagles with rubies, appraised at 260 pesos.

Another crystal box in the form of a star, appraised at 16 pesos.

An aventurine [9] cask with tap, appraised at 8 pesos.

A small aventurine ark with filigree metal springs, appraised at 10 pesos.

A small aventurine cask, with tap decorated with blue enamel and two little chains, appraised at 20 pesos.

The pieces of crystal and aventurine are worth (so it seems) 1,330 pesos according to the appraisal. What resulted from the raffle was 1,479 pesos, so that the amount was increased by 139 pesos above the appraisal.

1. The Vizarróns were powerful merchants and financiers from the area of the port complex of Cadiz and Puerto de Santa María in southern Spain. Luis Saenz de Tagle to Fausto de Bustamante and Juan Vizarrón, Power of attorney, Mexico City, 19 July 1696, Archivo General de Notarías de México, 692.

2. Black and red pottery, especially from Guadalajara in New Spain, was similar in appearance, workmanship, and fragrance to the Portuguese pottery so popular among the women at the Spanish court. Michaëlis de Vasconcellos *Algumas palavras*, 10, 51. Giovanni Francesco Gemelli Carreri, *Viaje a la Nueva España* (Mexico City, 1983), 1:19.

3. For five centuries, from the fourteenth until the nineteenth, the monastery of Guadalupe in the province of Cáceres was the most venerated religious shrine in Spain. Nuestra Señora de Guadalupe had been revered even longer in Seville, before A.D. 711, when the Moors invaded the Iberian Peninsula. Her image was taken to Guadalupe and buried to prevent her discovery and profanation by the infidels. Some time before 1327, she miraculously appeared and spoke to a cowherd, and her image was found. The Hieronymite Order established a monastery dedicated to Nuestra Señora de Guadalupe that soon became a center of Christian piety, culture, erudition, and the arts.

Soon after the fall of the Aztec capital of Tenochtitlan, the Franciscans built a shrine to the Virgin of the Apocalypse on Tepeyac Hill, a site associated with the pre-Conquest devotion to the goddess Tonantzin. Under the Franciscan's tutelage, an Indian painted an image of the Virgin at the shrine. Spanish visitors noted a remarkable similarity to the Virgin of Guadalupe in Spain and began to refer to her as Nuestra Señora de Guadalupe. The Franciscans attempted to squash the emerging cult, but Alonso de

Montúfar, the second archbishop of Mexico City, fostered it to weaken the control of the regular clergy over the indigenous population. Writing his *Imágen de la Vírgen María, Madre de Dios de Guadalupe* in 1648, Father Miguel Sánchez traced the origin of the cult to 1531 and a miraculous apparition to an Indian, Juan Diego.

On Friday 25 March 1695, the Day of Our Lady of the Assumption, the Conde de Galve and the Audiencia were present as Archbishop Francisco de Aguiar y Seijas laid the first stone at the basilica of Nuestra Señora de Guadalupe. Robles, *Diario*, 3:14. Colin M. MacLachlan and Jaime E. Rodríguez O., *The Forging of the Cosmic Race: A Reinterpretation of Colonial Mexico* (Berkeley, 1980):130–31. Carlos Callejo, *El Monasterio de Guadalupe* (Madrid, 1958):5–20.

4. Chocolate was introduced into Spain from New Spain in the 1520s. Though its use spread slowly throughout Europe, it triumphed completely in Spain, where it was recognized as a healthful stimulant. Chocolate was served, flavored with cinnamon, as a favorite drink in Madrid by the early seventeenth century. Long before Gelvira arrived in New Spain, the drinking of chocolate, flavored with sugar, cinnamon, vanilla, and anise, at five o'clock in the evening had become habitual.

Though chocolate made from cacao beans was established in the pre-Conquest Valley of Mexico, it was a prized import used as common currency and as a beverage by the privileged. The word and drink derive from *xocoatl*, an Aztec beverage made from corn, chile, and chocolate. In an interesting exercise in cultural exchange, Spaniards carried chocolate from America to Madrid, altered the recipe to their tastes, and returned it to other regions of the Americas. Fernand Braudel, *Capitalism and Material Life, 1400–1800*, trans. Miriam Kochan (New York, 1975):178–79.

Charles Gibson, *The Aztecs Under Spanish Rule: A History of the Indians of the Valley of Mexico, 1519–1810* (Stanford, 1964):348. José García Payón, *Amaxocoatl o libro del chocolate* (Toluca, 1936):12, 42.

5. Once trade between China and New Spain was established in the 1570s through Manila, Chinese fans, though fragile, figured among the earliest trade items. Often made from sandalwood or ivory, they were readily available in markets throughout the viceroyalty. William Lytle Schurz, *The Manila Galleon* (New York, 1939):33, 72. Gemelli Careri, *Viaje*, 17–18.

6. The Manila Galleon yearly plied the seas between Acapulco and Manila beginning in the early 1570s. In exchange for cargoes of silver (much sought after by the Chinese), cacao, cochineal, oil, and wine, the galleon brought to the viceroyalty a wide variety of luxury goods from the East. The largest component of the trade was silk, both clothing and yardage. There was also gold, jewelry (whose import was technically illegal), gems, spices, finely wrought bric-a-brac, and porcelain. Persian carpets, transhipped through India to Manila, were also included in this valuable commerce.

The Pacific passage was the longest and most perilous known to navigators. The trip from east to west, the most dangerous leg of the journey, lasted from five to seven months. Ships left Manila in June or July and reached Acapulco in December or January. Returning vessels departed New Spain late in February or early in March on a far easier sailing, usually arriving in the Philippines within three months.

The galleon for 1693, the *Santo Cristo de Burgos*, never arrived in New Spain. After leaving Manila, the ship burned at sea. Six men initially survived the sinking and escaped in a small open boat. Of the six, two were washed overboard and two managed to return to the Philippines—one insane, the other an admitted cannibal. Schurz, *Manila Galleon*, 32–33, 251–53, 259.

7. The cacao that supplied New Spain originated in three places: Central America, Venezuela, and Ecuador. Guatemala and Pacific Soconusco were significant sixteenth-century sources of the bean. Production declines in the seventeenth century, however, permitted the influx of cacao from Guayaquil and Venezuela. Despite this competition, Central America managed to maintain a foothold in the viceregal market, primarily because of its geographical proximity and an expanding market. A strong producer from the 1670s on, Venezuela also had to compete against the inferior, and cheaper, Ecuadorian bean in New Spain. By the end of the century, Venezuela had won this battle and firmly established itself as New Spain's "cacao colony." Robert J. Ferry, *The Colonial Elite of Early Caracas: Formation and Crisis, 1567–1767* (Berkeley, 1989):45–71. Eduardo Arcila Farías, *Comercio entre Venezuela y México en los siglos xvi y xvii* (Mexico City, 1950):56, 100. Murdo J. MacLeod, *Spanish Central America: A Socioeconomic History, 1520–1720* (Berkeley, 1973):235–45.

8. Carmona is a community in the province of Seville.

9. Aventurine is either glass with opaque sparkling particles, usually copper or chromic oxide, or translucent quartz with bright flakes of mica or other mineral.

23. The Condesa de Galve to the Marqués del Cenete, Mexico City, 4 June 1693, LS.

Most excellent lord,

My brother-in-law and lord, though in the last packet boat I wrote your excellency, I do so again now to solicit news of your excellency's health. I shall be happy if it as good as I wish and that my sister-in-law and nephews enjoy this benefit. I kiss their hands.

I remain ready to serve your excellency with my poor health somewhat improved, though not completely. It is a consolation to see my husband so far along. He has also suffered a considerable decline in his health. It is no small thing that he has improved despite his continual labor. See, your excellency, if I can serve you in some way. I shall do so with much pleasure. May Our Lord protect your excellency the many years I wish. Mexico City, 4 June 1693.

Most excellent lord, your sister-in-law and least servant kisses your excellency's hands,

Gelvira, the Condesa de Galve [rubrica]

Most excellent lord duque, the Duque and Marqués del Cenete, my brother-in-law and lord

24. THE CONDESA DE GALVE TO THE DUQUE DEL INFANTADO Y PASTRANA, MARQUÉS DEL CENETE, MEXICO CITY, 28 JUNE 1693, LS.

Most excellent sir,

My brother-in-law and lord, with the packet boat[1] that just arrived here from those kingdoms, I have received two letters from your excellency, the last dated last 11 February. Your excellency will know of the deep affection and love I professed for my sister-in-law (may she be in holy glory),[2] and how sorry I am that she is gone. I express my condolences to your excellency, assuring you I earnestly share your pain. The only thing that will alleviate mine is knowing that your excellency enjoys perfect health. I ask Our Lord that it will be so for many years. I remain to serve your excellency, somewhat recovered and wishing for Our Lord to protect you the many years He can. Mexico City, 28 June 1693.

Most excellent sir, your sister and greatest servant kisses your excellency's hands,

Gelvira, the Condesa de Galve [rubrica]

Most excellent lord duque, the Duque Marqués del Cenete, my brother and lord

1. On 23 June 1693, word that the packet boat had arrived reached Mexico City. The mail followed two days later. Robles, *Diario*, 2:290–91.

2. The Duquesa del Infantado died on 10 February 1693. Arteaga y Falguera, *Casa del Infantado*, 2:141–42.

25. The Condesa de Galve to Manuel de Silva y Mendoza, Mexico City, 25 June 1694, LS.

My nephew[1] and lord,

Having learned of the death[2] of my brother-in-law, the Duque del Infantado (may he be in glory), I cannot fail to fulfill my duty, extending my condolences to you for this loss, in which I have been so involved. In all sincerity, I join you in the understandable regret you will have felt. I hope that Our Lord will grant you extended good health and protect you many happy years. Mexico City, 25 June 1694.

Your aunt and least servant kisses your hand,

Gelvira, the Condesa de Galve [rubrica]

Lord don Manuel de Silva y Mendoza, my nephew and lord
Mexico City, 25 June 1694
For don Manuel, my lord, from the Condesa de Galve

1. Manuel de Silva y Mendoza was the second son of Gregorio and María. He was born on 18 October 1677. After the death of Gaspar he inherited his uncle's title, becoming tenth Conde de Galve. Arteaga y Falguera, *Casa del Infantado*, 2:128. Autos tocantes a la posesión del estado de Galve, Madrid, 17 Mar. 1697, AHPM, P. 12.118.

2. On 15 February 1694, a ship that had sailed from Spain on 4 October 1693 arrived in Veracruz with correspondence for the Conde de Galve, including notification of the death of his brother, the Duque del Infantado, on 10 September 1693. On 1 March, a ship from Santo Domingo repeated the news, and on the tenth, Galve honored his brother with a service in the Convento of San Francisco. Robles, *Diario,* 2:301–302. Arteaga y Falguera, *Casa del Infantado,* 2:144.

26. The Condesa de Galve to the Marqués de Távara, Mexico City, 26 June 1694, LS.

My brother and lord,

My affection does not allow missing an opportunity to write you by this packet boat,[1] which is being sent to those kingdoms. I am vexed at how much news from there has been delayed, since we have been a year without it. I have been without news of you for much longer for having stopped writing at every opportunity. I attribute this to the neglect of their not having sent you news from Madrid, and I must take into consideration your love for me. He who loves well does not soon forget.

I shall be happy if you enjoy perfect health in the company of my sister-in-law and Our Lord has given you a lengthy succession with the full congratulations my true affection and will offer you. I am very ill, suffering, my health broken because some abscesses[2] have suddenly erupted in a very sensitive place. They have kept me in bed more than a month, in great pain. I am now up and about and better (thanks be to God), though the wound is still open.

You can imagine how upset I am to be in

this kingdom when my heartfelt desire was that this year my husband's successor would come and we would be able to return as soon as possible. I have high hopes about this. Finally seeing you is my only wish; may Our Lord grant me this.

There is nothing new in particular here to tell you about. I beg you not to stop writing me whenever you have the opportunity, giving me this pleasure and that of telling me what might be offered you for yours. You know I shall obey you in everything with my affection and will. May God protect you many years as I wish and is so necessary for me. Mexico City, 26 June 1694.

My love, my poor health keeps me from writing you in my own hand and at length, but you should try to do so to soothe me.

Your sister who loves you and wishes to see you kisses your hands,

Gelvira [rubrica]

My brother and lord, the Marqués de Távara
Gelvira
Mexico City, 26 June 1694
My lady, the Condesa de Galve

1. The packet boat departed for Spain on 17 July 1694. Robles, *Diario*, 2:308.

2. Given this very brief description of symptoms, it is difficult to identify Gelvira's malady. The symptomatology is consistent with Bartholin abscesses, which involve glands situated near the labia. In the presence of bacterial exposure, commonly gonorrhea (but including other bacteria) the glands become inflamed and the ducts blocked. The result is a swelling of the labia, sometimes to the size of golf balls; the accompanying pain is excruciating. This conjectural diagnosis resulted from consultations with Nancy W. Wilking, M.D.

27. THE CONDESA DE GALVE TO THE MARQUÉS DE TÁVARA, MEXICO CITY, 5 JUNE 1696, ALS.

My brother and love of my life and heart,

On the occasion of my husband's dispatching this packet boat,[1] I tell you how excited I am to have received two letters from you. The most recent is from 28 June. Because you are well, all else is less important. I deeply regret than you are still stuck in that remote corner. I trust in God that we will all soon be able to hold our heads high.

God has seen fit for us to see one another with this fleet.[2] I assure you I am mad with joy. Though the way is difficult and very dangerous, I have no fear; rather my desire is to get on with it. I believe our departure from here will be around the first of May and from Veracruz[3] around the middle of June.

I trust in God that we shall see one another this year. For this reason, I do not plan to write at length. We are very hurried, as much to dispatch this packet boat as to make the preparations for our journey. We shall see each other and speak of the nine years here that we have not seen one another.

Here I want to say that the death of Brígida is a shame.[4] She married, and not to my satisfaction. She gave birth to a girl and died during childbirth.[5] I have the child in my home and am struggling to understand her. She is more that a year old, and I have to carry her nursing. She is as ugly as can be, but very much the joker.

There is nothing new here to tell you about. If there is, it will be when my husband leaves office.[6] I shall carry this news to you there, but what I shall not take is my maidservants.

There is a great rush to marry. One young woman you do not know married, as did one from my chamber. Two others are about to marry. One is doña Manuela,[7] and I greatly regret it because she will remain here. When we see each other, we shall speak of many things. I ask God that we achieve this. May his majesty protect you for me, love of my life, as is so necessary to me. Mexico City, 5 June 1696.

She who loves you most and is yours until death,

Gelvira [rubrica]

The Marqués de Távara, Mexico City, 5 June 1696

My lady, the Condesa de Galve

1. The packet boat sailed from Veracruz for Spain on 16 January 1696. Robles, *Diario*, 3:37.

2. Word that the fleet carrying Gaspar and Gelvira to Spain from Veracruz reached Mexico City on 11 August 1696. Robles, *Diario*, 3:49.

3. The new city of Veracruz, located on New Spain's eastern coast, was established in 1599 and replaced Villa Rica de Vera Cruz, the settlement Cortés had originally founded in 1519. It served as the principal port for ships coming from Spain and housed the customs house. Both the port and customs were controlled by the descendants of Cortés, the Marqueses del Valle.

Despite its maritime importance, the city was a miserable place, plagued by a terrible climate and high living expenses. Its air was considered unhealthy, particularly in the summer, when the weather was extremely hot. Lack of city walls made the settlement vulnerable to strong north winds, which often caused houses to be half-buried under blowing sand. Because of the sandy soil, proper cultivation of foodstuffs was difficult. As a result, most had to be brought to the city at some cost.

Throughout most of the year, the population was made up primarily of Blacks and mestizos. Spaniards came to the city only at the time of the fleet's arrival. Once their business was concluded, they escaped inland, because of both Vera Cruz's inhospitable climate and its reputation as a dangerous town.

Two presidial infantry companies were stationed at the port, in addition to a cavalry company of sixty horses, used to guard the beach at night. Half a league from the city was a fortress, which served to protect the harbor and ships anchored there. It enjoyed the natural defense of many reefs to both the east and west, which posed a considerable danger to unsuspecting ships.

Because of the city's poverty and small population, only one parish church and one Jesuit church could be supported. Gemelli Carreri, *Viaje*, 2:246–49.

4. Brígida de España was described as a chambermaid who accompanied the Conde de Galve and his family to New Spain. The Conde de Galve, Certification of the members of his household, Cadiz, 1 July 1688, AGI, Contratación 5450:47.

5. The perils of childbirth were well known to the medical profession. Propriety dictated that midwives, though neither examined nor licensed, handle births that presented no complications. Male physicians disdained obstetrics because it was associated with surgery and could therefore be practiced by those without university degrees. They were nevertheless called upon in the course of medical emergencies, such as breech birth. Furthermore, although practitioners understood at some level the importance of hygiene, they did not grasp the connection between disease and lack of sanitation.

No matter who supervised the birthing process, women always risked death by hemorrhaging or puerperal fever and, as aftereffects, bladder perforation, scabbing, prolapse of the womb, incontinence, and sciatica. Treatment for these conditions usually consisted of herbal remedies. Nicolás León, *La obstétrica en México* (Mexico City, 1910):200. John Leddy Phelan, *The Royal Protomedicato: The Regulation of the Medical Professions in the Spanish Empire* (Durham, 1985):298–99, 305. Hermosilla Molina, *Cien años*, 466–79.

6. Gelvira initiated her good-byes with a visit to the nunneries, beginning with the Capuchins, on 19 January. The Conde de Galve relinquished the viceroyalty on 21 January 1696. The first choice to replace him as interim viceroy was the bishop of Puebla,

Dr. Manuel Fernández de Santa Cruz. On 23 January, Fernández renounced the position and the second selection, Juan de Ortega Montañés, bishop of Michoacán was named viceroy. On 29 January, Ortega Montañés accepted the nomination. He arrived in Mexico City and Galve received him on 24 February. Three days later, after his official entry, he was received by the Cabildo, the Audiencia, the members of the various tribunals, and representatives at the cathedral. From there he proceeded to the palace where he took possession and swore the oath of office. At eleven o'clock, he went on to Galve's house. His day ended at the home of Antonio Flores, where he lodged. Robles, *Diario*, 3:36–39.

7. Manuela Rojo was a dama of the Galve household who accompanied the family from Spain. The Conde de Galve, Certification of the members of his household, Cadiz, 1 July 1688, AGI, Contratación 5450:47.

APPENDIX I

A la merced de alguna presea que la Excelentísima Señora doña Elvira de Toledo (Condesa de Galve), Virreina de Méjico, le presentó: corresponde con una Perla, y con este Romance, de no menor fineza, que envió desde Méjico a la Señora Condesa de Paredes.

¡Hermosa, divina Elvira,
a cuyas plantas airosas,
los que a Apolo son laureles
aun no les sirven de alfombra;
  a quien Venus y Minerva
reconocen, envidiosas,
la Ateniense, por más sabia,
la Cipria, por más hermosa;
  a quien se el Pastor Ideo
diera la dorada poma,
lo justo de la sentencia
le excusara la discordia,
  pues a vista del exceso
de tus prendas generosas,
sin esperar al examen
te cediera la corona!
  ¡Tú que impedirle pudieras
la tragedia lastimosa
a Andrómeda, y de Perseo
el asunto a la victoria,
  pues mirando tu hermosura
las Nereidas, ambiciosas,

su belleza despreciaran
y a tí te envidiaran sola!
   Ese concepto Oriental
que del llanto de la Aurora
concibió concha lucida,
a imitación de tu boca,
   en quien la Naturaleza,
del arte competidora,
siendo forma natural
finge ser artificiosa,
   quizá porque en su figura
erudición cierta y docta
a fascinantes contagios
da virtud preservadora,
   con justa razón ofrezco
a tus aras victoriosas,
pues por tributo del mar
a Venus sólo le toca.
   Bien mi obligación quisiera
que excediera, por preciosa,
a la que líquida en vino
engrandecí Egipcias bodas,
   o a aquélla que, blasón Regio
de la grandeza Española,
nuestros Católicos Reyes
guardan, vinculada joya.
   Pero me consuela el ver
que, si tu tocado adorna,
con prestarle tú el Oriente
será más rica que todas:

que el lucir tanto los Astros
que del Cielo son antorchas,
no es tanto por lo que son,
como donde se colocan.
　　Recíbela por ofrenda
de mi fineza amorosa,
pues para ser sacrificio
no en vano quiso ser hostia:
　　mientras yo, para la prenda
de tu mano generosa,
como para mejor perla,
del corazón hago concha.

Juana de Asbaje y Ramírez de Santillana [Sor Juana Inés de la Cruz (1651–95)], *Obras completas de Sor Juana Inés de la Cruz: I, Lírica personal,* ed. Alfonso Méndez Plancarte (Mexico City, 1951):117–19.

De pintura, no vulgar, *en ecos*, de la Excelentísima Señora Condesa de Galve, Virreina de Méjico.

El soberano Gaspar
par es de la bella Elvira:
vira de Amor más derecha,
hecha de sus armas mismas.
　　Su ensortijada medeja
deja, si el viento la enriza,
riza tempestad, que encrespa

crespa borrasca a las vidas.

De plata bruñida plancha,
ancha es campaña de esgrima;
grima pone el ver dos marcos,
arcos que mil flechas vibran.

Tiros son, con que de enojos,
ojos que al alma encamina,
mina el pecho, que cobarde
arde en sus hermosas iras.

Arbitro, a su parecer,
ser la nariz determina:
termina dos confinantes,
antes que airados se embistan.

De sus mejillas el campo
ampo es, que con nieve emprima
prima labor, y la rosa
osa resaltar más viva.

De sus labios, el rubí
vi que color aprendía;
prendía, teniendo ensartas,
sartas dos de perlas finas.

Del cuello el nevado torno,
horno es, que incendios respira;
pira en que Amor, que renace,
hace engaños a la vista.

Triunfos son, de sus dos palmas,
almas que a su sueldo alista;
lista de diez alabastros:
Astros que en su cielo brillan.

En lo airoso de su talle,

halle Amor su bizarría;
ría de que, en el donaire,
aire es todo lo que pinta.
   Lo demás, que bella oculta,
culta imaginaria admira;
mira, y en lo que recata, ata el labio, que peligra.

Sor Juana, *Obras completas*, 1:119–20.

A la misma Señora (la Condesa de Galve), en ocasión de cumplir años.

Si el día en que tú naciste,
bellísima, excelsa Elvira,
es ventura para todos,
¿por qué no lo será mía?
   ¿Nací yo acaso en las yerbas,
o criéme en las hortigas?
¿Fué mi ascendiente algún risco,
o mi cuna alguna sima?
¿No soy yo gente? ¿No es forma
racional la que me anima?
¿No desciendo, como todos,
de Adán por mi recta línea?
   ¿No hay sindéresis en mí
con que lo mejor elija,
y ya que bien no lo entienda
por lo menos lo perciba?
   ¿Pues por qué no he de ir a verte

cuando todos te visitan?
¿Soy ave nocturna para
no poder andar de día?

Si porque estoy encerrada
me tienes por impedida,
para estos impedimentos
tiene el afecto sus limas.

Para el alma no hay encierro
ni prisiones que la impidan,
porque sólo la aprisionan
las que se forma ella misma.

Sutil y ágil el deseo,
no hay, cuando sus plumas gira,
solidez que no penetre
ni distancia que no mida.

Mejorados van mis ojos
cuando a verte se destinan,
pues para que ellos te vean
retiró el alma la vista.

Contento con mi carencia
mi respeto, sacrifica,
por el culto que te doy,
el gusto que se me priva.

Entre el gusto y el decoro
quiere la razón que elija
lo que es adoración tuya
antes que la fruición mía.

Yo me alegro de no verte,
porque fuera grosería
que te cueste una indecencia

el que yo logre una dicha.

   A objeto tanto, ella sola
llegará menos indigna,
porque nunca a la Deidad
los ojos mortales miran.
Allá voy a verte; pero
perdóname la mentira:
que mal puede ir a un lugar
el que siempre en él habita.

   Yo siempre de tu asistencia
soy la mental estantigua,
que te asisto y no me sientes,
que te sirvo y no me miras.

   Yo, envidiosa de la Esfera
dichosa que tú iluminas,
formo de mis pensamientos
las alfombras que tú pisas;

   y aunque invisible, allí el alma
te venera tan rendida,
que apenas logra el deseo
desperdicios de tu fimbria.

   Mas cierto, que del asunto
estoy más de cuatro millas,
que leguas dijera, a no
ser el asonante en *ía*.

   Revístome de dar años,
que aunque tan no apetecida
dádiva en las Damas, es
de la que tú necesitas,

   pues es tan breve el espacio

de tu juventud florida,
que a otras se les darán años,
pero a ti se te dan días.

Yo te los doy; y no pienses
que voy desapercibida
de las alhajas que observa
hoy la etiqueta precisa.

Pues si de los años es
una cadena la insignia,
yo tengo la de tu esclava;
mira si hay otra más rica.

Por joyel, un corazón
que en vez de diamantes brilla
el fondo de mi fineza,
el resplandor de mi dicha.

Góceslos como deseo,
como mereces los vivas,
que en lo que quiero y mereces
dos infinitos se cifran:

que, pues vives de lucir,
de los lustros la medida
(pues que se dijo *a lustrando*)
sólo en tí se verifica.

No quiero cansarte más,
porque de que estés es día
hermosa a más no poder
y de adrede desabrida.

Sor Juana, *Obras completas*, 1:120–23.

A la misma Excelentísima Señora (la Condesa de Galve), hallándola superior a cualquier elogio.

Sobre si es atrevimiento,
bella Elvira, responderte,
y sobre si también era
cobardía el no atreverme,
   he pasado pensativa,
sobre un libro y un bufete
(porque vayan otros *sobres*),
sobre el amor que me debes,
   no sé yo qué tantos días;
porque como tú en ti tienes
reloj de Sol, no hay quien mida
lo que vive o lo que muere.
   Y si no lo has por enojo,
después que estaba el caletre
cansado asaz de pensar
y de revolver papeles,
   resuelta a escribirte ya,
en todos los aranceles
de Jardines y de Luces,
de Estrellas y de Claveles,
   no hallé en luces ni colores
comparación conveniente,
que con más de quince palmos
a tu hermosura viniese,
   con ser que no perdoné
trasto que no revolviese

en la tienda de Timantes
ni en el obrador de Apeles.
    Pues a los Poetas, ¡cuánto
les revolví los afeites
con que hacen que una hermosura
dure aunque al tiempo le pese!
    En Petrarca hallé una copia
de una Laura, o de una duende,
pues dicen que sér no tuvo
más del que en sus versos tiene.
    Cubierta, como de polvo,
de Griego, una copia breve
hallé de Elena, de Homero
olvidada en un retrete.
    Pues de Virgilio el coturno
no dejó de enternecerse
con Elisa, en el *quam lae-*
ti te genuere parentes.
    A Proserpina, en Claudiano,
ni aun me dió gana de verle
la su condenada faz,
llena de hollines y peces.
    De Lucrecia la Romana,
aquella beldad valiente
persuadiendo honor estaba
a las Matronas de allende.
    Florinda vana decía
a los moros alquiceles:
Tanto como España valgo,
pues toda por mí se pierde.

Lavinia estaba callada
dejando, que allá se diesen
Turno y el *pater* Eneas,
y después: ¡Viva quien vence!

En Josefo Marïamne,
al ver que sin culpa muere,
dijo: Si me mata Herodes,
claro es que estoy Inocente.

Angélica, en Arïosto,
andaba de hueste en hueste
alterando Paladines
y descoronando Reyes.

En Ovidio, como es
Poeta de las Mujeres,
hallé que al fin los pintares
eran como los quereres;

y hallé a escoger, como en peras,
unas bellezas de a veinte,
a lo de *¿qué queréis, pluma?*,
que están diciendo *comedme*,

en los prados, más que flores,
en el campo, más que nieves,
en las plantas, más que frutos,
y en las aguas, más que peces.

A la rubia Galatea
junto a la cándida Tetis,
a la florida Pomona
y a la chamuscada Ceres;

a la gentil Aretusa
y a la música Canente,

a la encantadora Circe
y a la desdichada Heles;
  a la adorada Coronis,
y a la infelice Semele,
a la agraciada Calisto,
y a la jactante Climene,
  y a otra gran tropa de Ninfas
acuátiles y silvestres,
sin las Mondongas, que a aquéstas
guardaban los adherentes;
  a la desdeñosa Dafne,
a la infausta Nictimene,
a la ligera Atalanta
y a la celebrada Asterie;
  y en fin, la Casa del Mundo,
que tantas pinturas tiene
de bellezas vividoras,
que están sin envejecerse,
  cuya dura cama, el Tiempo,
que todas las cosas muerde
con los bocados de siglos,
no les puede entrar el diente,
  revolví, como ya digo,
sin que entre todas pudiese
hallar una que siquiera
en el vestido os semeje.
  Con que, de comparaciones
desesperada mi mente,
al *¿viste?* y al *así como*
hizo ahorcar en dos cordeles,

ya sin tratar de pintarte,
sino sólo de quererte:
porque ésta, aunque culpa, es culpa
muy fácil de cometerse,

   y esotra, imposible y culpa;
y a más de culpa, se temen
de Icaro los precipicios
y de Faetón los vaivenes.

   Mira qué vulgar ejemplo,
que hasta los niños de leche
faetonizan e icrizan
la vez que se les ofrece.

   Y en fin, no hallo qué decirte,
sino sólo que ofrecerte,
adorando tus favores,
las gracias de tus mercedes.

   De ellos me conozco indigna;
mas eres Sol, y amaneces
por beneficio común
para todos igualmente.

   Por ellos, Señora mía,
postrada beso mil veces
la tierra que pisas y
los pies, que no sé si tienes.

Sor Juana, *Obras completas*, 1:123–26.

A la misma Excelentísima Señora (la Condesa de Galve), enviándole un Zapato bordado, según estilo de Méjico, y un recado de Chocolate.

> Tirar el guante, Señora,
> es señal de desafío;
> con que tirar el zapato
> será muestra de rendido.
>   El querer tomar la mano
> es de atrevemiento indicio;
> pero abatirse a los pies,
> demostración de rendido.
>   Bien es que, en los vuestros, se
> falsifica este principio,
> pues se sube en la substancia
> y se baja en el sonido.
>   Que subir a vuestras plantas,
> es intento tan altivo,
> que aun se ignora en lo elevado
> la noticia del peligro.
>   Ni del que osó temerario
> circundar el azul giro,
> ni del que al Planeta ardiente
> cera y pluma oponer quiso,
>   pudiera dar la rüina
> escarmentados avisos;
> que no sirven de ejemplares
> inferiores precipicios.
>   Pero ¿a dónde me remonto?
> Ya parece que los sigo,

pues tan fuera del intento
iba torciendo el camino.

   Digo, que el día, Señora
de aquel Santísimo Obispo
en quien no fueron milagros
los milagros, por continuos,

   como es día de licor,
éste, aunque no muy bendito,
pues en señal de su origen
lleva el *pulvis es* escrito,

   os envía cierto afecto,
que viendo que sois prodigio
de la beldad, por milagro
presume que el Santo os hizo.

   En ir tan corto el regalo,
va a su dueño parecido;
que al que a los suyos parece,
bendice un refrán antiguo.

   Por aquesto va, Señora,
tan cobarde y tan sumiso,
que pienso, que el mismo Amor
lo dejó por escondido.

   Hasta el recado tasado
va, tan mudo y sin rüido,
que van guardando secreto
las ruedas del molinillo.

   Porque quien es, quiere, haciendo
de Amor verdadero oficio,
pues sois Psiquis en belleza,
que no ignoréis que hay Cupido;

pero no que sepáis cuál;
que fuera necio capricho,
entre desaires de corto,
hacer alardes de fino.

Yo os debo servir, y así
ya sé que en servir no obligo,
ni hago la deuda obsequio
ni de la paga servicio.

Como no sabéis quién soy,
a la cortedad me animo,
que no hay color en el rostro
cuando está callado el pico.

Así lo pienso tener;
porque solamente cifro
la vanidad de adoraros
en la gloria de serviros.

Sor Juana, *Obras completas*, 1:127–28.

Appendix 2

Doñas and Ladies

Doña Magdalena de Villegas Retes
Doña Tomasa Fernando
Doña Bernarda de Torres
Doña María Catalina de Torres
Doña Manuela Rojo
Doña Teresa de Torres
Doña Magdalena de las Cuevas
Doña Antonia de Silva y Toledo
Doña Alfonsa de Fonseca Piña
Doña Estefanía de Vozmediano

Chambermaids

Margarita del Castillo
Agüeda de la Higuera
Ana Rufel
Brígida de España
Isabel

Servants

Father Alonso de Quirós, S.J., Galve's confessor
    Father Manuel Navarro, coadjutor, his companion
Don Antonio Salvago, Galve's chaplain
    José de Losada, his servant

Don Amadeo Isidro Zeyol, Galve's mayordomo
    Ignacio Ceballos, his servant
Don Juan Francisco de Vargas, Galve's secretary
    Doña Josefa Prehón, his wife
    Francisco Gómez, his servant
Don Pedro de Leyva, Galve's equerry
    Doña Mencia de Orozco, his wife; don Gaspar, don Pedro,
    and Doña Micaela de Leyva, his children
Doña Francisca Argüero, servant of don Pedro de Leyva
Don Pedro Manuel de Torres
    Doña Margarita Valenzuela, his wife
Don Martín Cruerso, Galve's doctor
    Alonso de la Cruz, his servant
Esteban de Torres, Galve's surgeon
    Andrés de Jimeno, his servant

Gentlemen of the Bedchamber

Don Diego Morales, Chambermaster
Don Sebastian de Ugarte
Don Juan Cortés
Don Juan Briones
Don Antonio Pariente
Don Fernando de Bustamante
Don Antonio de Orejón
Don Bartolomé de Torres

Appendix 2

Pages

Don Alonso López de Barreda
Don Matías Gutiérrez de Espina
Don Pedro de la Barreda
Don Gerónimo de Celada
Don Diego de Celada
Don Francisco Aldado
Don Francisco Palomegue
Don Mateo de Sobrevilla
Don Juan Galdo
Don Manuel de Alvarado
Don José de Valladolid
Don Miguel Pérez de San Pedro
Diego Bermúdez, pages' servant

Oficials of the Secretariat

Don Antonio de Mata
    Doña Manuela de Parla y Olmedo, his wife
Don Manuel Tirado
Don Manuel López de Rojas

Chamber aids

Matías González
    Doña Frailana García, his wife
    Doña María García, her sister
    Juan Antonio González, his son
Andrés de Otero, barber

Francisco Pérez, tailor
Cosme Corne
 Doña Inés Vélez, his wife

Tradesmen and -women

Lázaro Piedra, overseer
Benito Díaz, valet
 Mariana Rodríguez, his wife
Juan Arias, keeper of the drawing-room
 Isabel Gámez, his wife
Santiago González, mozo de retrete
 Isabel López de Parga, his wife
Antonio Fernández, butler
 Juan Molero and Antonio Presto, his assistants
Esteban García, chef
Pedro Fernández and Juan Ezequiel, his assistants and
Pedro Fernández, his nephew

AGI, Contratación 5450:47

APPENDIX 3

Members of the Sagrario Metropolitano Parish residing in the house of the Marquéses del Valle, 1695

The most excellent lord, the Conde de Galve
The most excellent lady, the Condesa de Galve
Don Antonio Salvago
Don Felipe de la Carrera
Doña Magdalena de Villegas [Retes]
Doña Tomasa Fernando
Doña María Catalina [de Torres]
Doña Manuela Rojo
Doña Antonia de Silva y Toledo
Doña Estefanía de Vozmediano
Margarita del Castillo
Agüeda de la Higuera
Ana Rufel
Paula de Villegas
Francisca de Padilla
Don Juan Cortés
Don Pedro de Leyva
Don Amadeo Isidro Zeyol
Don Diego Morales
Don Alonso [López] de Barreda
Don Antonio Terán
Don Rafael Cortés
Don Miguel de Santa Cruz
Don Gerónimo [de] Celada

Appendix 3

Don Diego [de] Celada
Don Pedro Manuel de Torres
Don Manuel Tirado
Don Antonio de Mata
Don José de Valladolid
Don Mateo de Sobrevilla
Don Nicolás de Fonseca
Don Gaspar de Leyva
Don José de Marino
Don Luis Ibáñez
Patricio de Soto Carrillo
Cosme Corne
Andrés [de] Otero
Benito Díaz
Domingo El Chino
Santiago González
Juan Arias
Tomás González
Don Felipe de Santoya
Lázaro Piedra
Francisco Gerónimo
Juan Molero
José Antonio
Pedro Fernández
Juan Ezequiel
Juan de Bonhora
The kitchen boy
The ladies' servant
The pages' servant
José [de] Losada

María del Campo
Nicolasa de la Caridad
Juliana de San Juan
The mistress who brought the daughter of don Pedro de
    Leyva
The three little French children
Francisco Ferreira
Agustín de Otero
José de Tovar
José de Sandía
Juan de Dios
José de Velasco
Pedro Mansilla
Tomás Ochoa
Juan Bautista
Pedro Hidalgo
Antonio del Campo
José de Rivera
Miguel de Moncada
Gregorio Mansilla
Carlos de Quivira
Juan de Seles
Diego de Santiago
Gregorio Simón
Domingo del Campo
Nicolás de Figueroa
Matías Guerrero
Esteban de la Cruz
Juan Antonio
José de Flores

Appendix 3

Domingo de Mendoza
Tomás de Sandía
Juan de Monsalve
Felipe de Santiago
Domingo, bugler
Pedro Hidalgo, bugler

LDS: Sagrario Metropolitano, Mexico City, List of members, 1695, microfilm 0036415

Appendix 4
Spanish Transcripts

Note on Symbols

1. Editorial expansions of abbreviations are indicated by italics.

2. Text enclosed by square brackets and carets ([^]) indicates changes to a hand other than the original hand.

3. Line lengths correspond to original Spanish line lengths. Lines exceeding typeset length end with a virgule (/).

1. The Condesa de Galve to the Marqués del Cenete, Madrid, n.d., ALS.

[fol. 1r]
q*ue*rido de mi bida y de mi co-
racon es ynposible ponderar-
te el gran gusto q*ue* he recibido
de ber letra tuya q*ue* en mi desconsuelo eso solo me podia a-
libiar aunq*ue h*asta q*ue* te buelba
a ber no *h*abra consuelo para
mi porq*ue* cada y*n*stante se au-
menta en lugar de conso-

larme y solo el considerarte
tan gustoso me causa alguno
por*que* si no fuera ese me mu-
era y asi lo q*ue* te pido es q*ue* no te
acuerdes de cosa q*ue* te de pesar
sino solo de lo q*ue* ha de ser gusto
tuyo y de mi hermana que en
lo q*ue* esta gocando *h*a sido
bien dichosa yo bien des-
[fol. 1v]
graciada q*ue*rido de mi bida
mi tio sera me escribio diçi-
endome q*ue* despachaba a gua-
darama y con eso no he q*ue*-
rido degar de molestarte
por darme yo a mi el ali-
bio de el rato q*ue* te escribia
por*que* no tengo otro y q*ue* te aseguro no le espero tener *h*asta
q*ue* te buelba a ber q*ue* me pareçe
*h*a cien años q*ue* no te beo y no
crey q*ue* te queria tanto como
te quiero no te quiero ser mas
molestia q*ue* en esta bida te lo
*h*e sido *h*arto q*ue*rido de mi bida no deges de mandarme
todo lo q*ue* gustares desde
alla q*ue* te aseguro solo eso me
alibiara mi dolor el ber q*ue*
te acuerdes de mi pues para

mayor martirio mio me per-
suado a q*ue* no lo has de *h*açer y
ya sabes con el gusto y pun-
tualidad q*ue* te obedeçere
[fol. 2r]
q*ue* no tengo q*ue* encarecerte lo
mas de lo q*ue* tu sabes sino q*ue* por
mi desdicha se te *h*aya ya olbidado q*ue* con tus glorias
no sera mucho se te *h*ayan
olbidado unas cosas de
tan poco probecho y eso solo
me traspasare a el alma
perdona estas sinplecas
q*ue* llebada solo de mi cariño y sentimiento y ya beo
q*ue* no nos *h*onraron pero tu
lo perdonaras con otras cosas mi primo me *h*a dicho
q*ue* no te hescribe por no en-
baracarsete y q*ue* lo *h*ara a Valladolid y yo tanbien y
en el interin zede dios muy
buen camino çolo como yo
desseo q*ue h*arto me *h*olgara yo de
ber las cartas todas tus criadas un abraco y las mias se po-
nen a tus pies
quien mas q*ue* a su
vida te quiere y desea ber

gelvira [rubrica]

2. The Condesa de Galve to the Marqués del Cenete, Madrid,
2 January 1688, AL.

[fol. 1r]
q*ue*rido de mi bida y de mi coraçon aunq*ue* este coreo no he teni*do*
carta tuya no escuso por es-
ta decirte q*ue* me *h*olgare de
q*ue* estes bueno y q*ue* sea floge-
dad y no otro motibo ya estoy
para serbirte estimandote
segunda bez lo rica q*ue* me tienes
q*ue* ya sabes tu q*ue* para mi basta-
ba ser tuyo sin tener los mo-
tibos q*ue* tienes q*ue*rido de mi
bida mateo me digo le di-
gese a Don pedro de castro q*ue*
tu decias q*ue* de los diez mil
reales q*ue* le *h*abian de traer
de la encomienda le *ha*-
bia de dar a el los seys y
a mi los cuatro y diçe q*ue*
[fol. 1v]
es menester q*ue* tu le enbies
unos libramientos para
q*ue* el pueda dar recibo y q*ue* ya
te lo tiene escrito q*ue*rido de
mi bida en esto be lo q*ue* gus-

tares de *h*açer y no me tengas
ociosa en tu serbicio a mi
hermana beso las m*a*n*o*s y
nuestro s*eñ*or me los *guard*e a entran-
bos mas q*ue* a mi m*a*d*ri*d y
henero a 2 de *1688*
quien mas q*ue* a su bida
te quiere y desea ber
brabas diligencias
se *h*acen sobre q*ue* se case luis con la del
Carpio reynante
otro coreo te escri-
bire mas despacio

3. The Condesa de Galve to the Marqués del Cenete, Madrid,
10 January 1688, ALS.

[fol. 1r]
q*ue*rido de mi bida te aseguro
q*ue* me tienes con grandisimo
cuydado el ber la dilacion
q*ue* tienen tus cartas pues
a dos coreos q*ue* no la tengo
y *h*asta lograr este gusto estare como puedes conside-
rar dios quiera *h*açerme
este beneficio y a ti te suplico no deges de escribir-
me aunq*ue* no sean mas q*ue* dos

letras diciendome como estas bueno y mi hermana
y haç me gusto de decirme
si es berdad que esta preña-
da porque me lo han dicho
algunas personas que lo
sabian de muy cierto y yo
[fol. 1v]
no lo he oueido porque el no
haberme tu dicho nada no
me parecia te deberia yo
tanpoco que ya sabes soy de
secreto y asi no deges de
abisarme si es cierto que hasta saberlo estoy con gran
rabia contigo por si has hecho
conmigo bella queria se-
megante querido mio por
mayor te quiero decir co-
mo mi padre esta muy
orgulloso en que mi hermano luys se ha de casar con
la del carpio y ha hecho di-
ferentes diligencias y
yo le he dicho hartas cosas
tocantes a todos por ber
la priesa que tiene y a mi me
hace tanta merçed que todo
lo comunica con nosotros
y no sabemos que quiera

[fol. 2r]

ser q*ue* asi mi primo como
yo estamos muy espanta-
dos de ber las confianças
sin merecerse las al fin
este negocio esta en manos
del conde de melgar
te yre abisando de lo q*ue*
fuere suçediendo pero
no se que te diga del efec-
to porq*ue* el conde es medio
loco y la marquesa madre
bariable como tu sabes
dios le g*uard*e y te me g*uard*e mas
q*ue* a mi m*adri*d y henero a 10 de
1688
no te des por entendido
con nayde de por aca
quien mas q*ue* a su bida
te estima y dessea ber
gelvira [rubrica]

4. The Condesa de Galve to the Marqués del Cenete, Madrid,
17 January 1688, ALS.

[fol. 1r]

q*ue*rido de mi bida y de mi
coraçon aunq*ue* no he tenido carta tuya no puedo degar de
ponerme a tu obediencia y

darte los dias de *h*oy con el
gusto q*ue* no puedes dudar
de mi cariño de q*ue* los lo-
gres como tanto hemos
deseado en conpañia
de mi hermana q*ue* anbos
creeran los celebrare con
mi q*ue* tu los cunples y q*ue* sean
tantos q*ue* no tengan nume-
ro y *h*açme merçed de dar-
selos a mi hermana y tra-
ta de escribirme y largo
n*ue*st*r*o *señ*or te me *guard*e mas q*ue* a mi m*adri*d
y 17 de *1*688
quien mas q*ue* a su bida
te quiere y dessea ber
gelvira [rubrica]

5. The Condesa de Galve to the Marqués del Cenete, Madrid,
31 January 1688, ALS.

[fol. 1r]
q*ue*rido de mi bida y de mi coraçon no me *h*arto de dar gracias a
Dios de q*ue* me *h*as aguado del susto en q*ue* nos *h*a tenido de no tener
cartas tuyas cuatro coreos ha
pero ya descanse con la tuya de
14 q*ue* no quiero encarecerte mas
mi desconsuelo q*ue* era berme sin

carta tuya y mi tia la de cabra
*h*aber dicho q*ue* estabas malo y
si me fuera posible *h*aberme ydo
a pie lo h*u*viera *h*echo de muy buena gana q*ue h*asta q*ue* sepa estas del
todo libre del dolor de cabeça
estare como tu puedes creer
y sienpre con el susto de el gran
frio q*ue h*ace por alla y considerando el gran calor del bera-
no q*ue* te aseguro para q*ue* yo tenga en todos tienpos la mortificacion de q*ue* estes ay y lo q*ue* te su-
[fol. 1v]
plico es q*ue* me digas muy por esten-
co lo q*ue* tienes q*ue* el no *h*acerlo es tener-
me colgada de los cabellos pero
creo me *h*agas esta merçed y la pon-
dre en lugar principas de las q*ue*
te he debido y debo y no te digo
mas sino q*ue* te acuerdes de lo q*ue*
te quiero y de q*ue* estoy ausente q*ue* esto solo te bastara para mirarme
como a mi mira si es mala la ba-
nidad q*ue* tengo y tu tienes la culpa q*ue*rido mio me diçes q*ue* no sea
tan agradeada y no se si me lo
diçes por ironia pues si tu sabes
q*ue* no esprimento de nayde lo q*ue*
detiene ausencia y en presencia

no es mucho q*ue* te lo agradeçca
como si fuera cien mil ducados
q*ue* para mi estimacion las son y
bien esto poco tengo yo q*ue* ponderar-
te pues sabes es cosa tuya para mi
y asi lo q*ue* te suplico es no me tengas
ociosa en tu serbicio n*ue*stro *se*ñor te me *guard*e
mas q*ue* a mi m*adri*d y henero a 31 de *1688*
quien mas q*ue* a su bida te
quiere y dessea ber
gelvira [rubrica]
no quiero de-
gar de decirte
q*ue* la boda de la
hija de la del
carpio esta ya
ajustada con
don fran*cis*co de
toledo conside-
ra a nuestro
licenciado
el coreo q*ue* bie-
ne te escribi-
re sobre esto
mas largo

6. The Condesa de Galve to the Marqués del Cenete, Madrid, 11 February 1688, ALS.

[fol. 1r]

querido de mi bida y de mi
coraçon aunque me *h*allo sin
carta tuya no quiero de-
gar de cansarte con es-
tos dos renglones sinni-
ficadote lo que me morti-
ficas a no escribirme
pero considerando si
te sirbe de molestia no
te aprieto mas y como
estes bueno que es lo que yo he
menester y asi no te qui-
ero cansar mas a mi
hermana beso las m*a*nos y
nuestro señor te me *guarde* mas que a mi
m*a*dri*d* y frebrero a 11 de *1688*
quien mas que a su be-
da te quiere y dessea ber
gelvira [rubrica]

7. The Condesa de Galve to the Marqués del Cenete, Madrid,
18 February 1688, ALS.

[fol. 1r]
querido de mi bida y de mi co-
racon mucho me *h*oguelo yo de
que estes ya tan megorado
que he estado sin saber de mi
y lo que te pido es que te cuydes mucho que ya sabes eres delica-

do y que cualquiera cosa te
haçe mal y asi te pido te guar-
des lo que me diere dares el lugar
de si del frio y del calor que aunque pienso no sera posible hasta
salir del en el interin da-
me a mi este consuelo que en la
ausencia que padezco de mi
galan no tengo otro sino es
saber esta bueno querido de
mi bida confiada en lo
que te debo me atrebo a supli-
carte me hagas gusto de enbi-
[fol. 1v]
ar a hacer a portugal unas
salbilla de baro colorado que
sea gordo y ellas de la hechura
de las del chocolate con aqua
hoyo en medio para la gica-
ra que se lo dige el otro dia a
un bareo y no quiso encar-
garse desto y asi te canso
que ya sabes lo tengo de haçer
siempre que se me ofreçca y ya
conozco es gran enpertinen-
cia faboreciendome como
tu me faboreçes pero contigo
no hay cumplimientos y tanbien me enbiaras unos pocos
de baros de beber u de las hec-

huras q*ue* gustares q*ue* sean los
mas gruesos q*ue* se pudiesen q*ue*-
rido mio ya le dige a mi
primo lo q*ue* me mandas-
te y el te respondera con
mas raçon lo q*ue* me dio sobre q*ue* el conde de tabara no
[fol. 2r]
le parecia q*ue* *h*aria lo q*ue* tu le
pedias de enbiar las prue-
bas a la persona señalada
q*ue* lo q*ue* *h*aria era enbiarlas
a los lugares q*ue* mandas pero a personas q*ue* no fuesen
señaladas por el sugeto
porq*ue* en esto y en todo *h*açe muy
recto presidente *h*arto me
*h*olgara yo asi q*ue* estubiese
en mi mano para serbir-
te q*ue* ya sabes tengo desseo de
darte gusto como lo espri-
mentaras sienpre q*ue* te a-
cuerdes de mandarme
a mi hermana beso las
manos y n*ue*s*t*ro se*ño*r me los g*ua*rde mas
q*ue* a mi m*a*dri*d* y febrero a 18 de
1688
quien mas q*ue* a su
vida te quiere y desseo ver
gelvira [rubrica]

Appendix 4

8. The Condesa de Galve to the Marqués del Cenete, Madrid,
6 March 1688, ALS.

[fol. 1r]
querido de mi bida y de mi coraçon mucho me holgare de que
estes bueno y mi hermana
a quien beso las manos y el
no haberte escrito estos dias ha sido por haber estado
sangrada de mi achaque
que aunque no eche abundan-
cia escupi una poca de san-
gre y con eso no me atrevido
a escribir por tener tan su-
mamente caliente la ca-
beça que estaba como una
loca querido de mi bida
te estimo como debo lo re-
galada que me tienes con
tan lindo salmon que no he
[fol. 1v]
bisto cosa mas linda y ya
estaba un poquito enogada
de que no te huvieses acorda-
do de mi habiendo enbia-

do salmon a madrid pe-
ro no *h*ay cosa q*ue* yo no te deba
de todas maneras mira
si tu gustas de alguna cosa de por aca q*ue* ya sabes soy
tuya aunq*ue* no me quieras
n*uest*ro se*ñ*or te me *guard*e mas q*ue* a mi
m*adri*d y marzo a 6 de *1*688
quien mas q*ue* a si
te quiere y dessea ber
gelvira [rubrica]

9. The Condesa de Galve to the Marqués del Cenete, Madrid,
13 March 1688, ALS.

[fol. 1r]
q*ue*rido de mi bida y de mi
coraçon este correo he tenido
carta tuya q*ue h*a sido para mi
de tan gran gusto y consuelo como puedes creer por haber
tanto tiempo q*ue* no la tenia y
en sabiendo yo q*ue* estas bueno
estoy con el gusto q*ue* puedes
considerar pues soy contigo
dos cuerpos y un alma aunq*ue*
tu no quieras q*ue*rido de
mi bida te buelbo a estimar
de nuebo lo rica q*ue* me tienes
por *h*aberlo cobrado a*h*ora

que al fin no hay cosa en este
mundo que yo no te deba y
no es mero en ti que hagas
estas demostraciones con-
migo ya sabes que de todas
[fol. 1v]
maneras soy mas tuya que mia
ni de nayde y te estimo los
baros que no hay carta en que no
tenga que estimarte y ya sabes que en esto de baros te tengo de cansar mucho por
gustar tanto de ellos pues
te trato con tanta llane-
ça que aunque conozco no es raçon en acordandome de
que eres tu mi cariño no permite cumplimiento mio
el no haberte escrito estos
coreos ha sido la causa tener
la cabeça de modo que no
me he atrebido y con la san-
gria que me hiçe se me mego-
ro tanto que puedo decir estoy buena y bien podia considerar que si no era esta ocasion no podia ser otra el
faltarte carta mia por-
[fol. 2r]
que yo no tenga otro consue-

lo en esta bida si no el de escribirte y que me escribas
y asi no te canses y mas con
lo que le escribiste a mi primo de que si queriamos cores-
pondencia todas las se-
manas las sobrescribi-
esemos a montiano no
digo yo cada semana
sino cada dia y cada ynstan-
te y a dios que no te quiero
cansar mas nuestro señor te me guarde mas que a mi
madrid y março
a 13 de 1688
quien mas que a su bi-
da te quiere y dessea ber
gelvira [rubrica]

10. The Condesa de Galve to the Marqués del Cenete, Madrid,
20 March 1688, ALS.

[fol. 1r]
querido de mi bida y de mi
coraçon aunque este coreo me
hallo sin carta tuya no me
admiro por el tienpo tan
malo que hace pero no quiero
degar de ponerme a tu obediencia por esta aunque sea
corta diciendote que estoy

buena y no me pareçe escu-
sable por lo que te debo aunque sea cansarte querido mio
te hago saber como se me ha cau-
sado ysabel solano y por-
que sepas aun cosas de tan poca ynportancia en siendo
dependientes de mi casa
no puedo degar de darte
cuenta ella se pone a tus pies y a los de mi herma-
na a quien beso las manos
[fol. 1v]
y ella y tu saben que estoy aqui
con tan buena boluntad
como siempre nuestro señor te me
guarde querido de mi bida mas
que a mi madrid y março a 20
de 1688
quien mas que a su
bida te quiere y dessea ber
gelvira [rubrica]

11. The Condesa de Galve to the Marqués del Cenete, Madrid,
7 April 1688, ALS.

[fol. 1r]
querida de mi bida aunque no
he tenido Carta tuya mucho
tiempo ha no escuso Cansarte

Con la mia significando Cu-
anto me *h*olgare de q*ue* estes
bueno yo lo estoy pero no sin
poca mortificacion de *h*aber-
te de dar Cuenta Como a mi
primo le *h*a *h*onrado el Rey Con
lo mas lejos q*ue* tenia q*ue* dar
pues le dio el bireyna-
to de mejico de q*ue* lo qual
no puedo dejar de serbir-
me de tan gran ternura
Como puedes Considerar
pues no puedo dejar a mi
primo ni me puedo lle-
bar un todo y no me ser-
[fol. 1v]
bira de poca el *h*aberme de
desterar tantas leguas
sin tener el Consuelo de
berte y a mi *h*ermana *h*oy te
pido se lo digas de mi parte q*ue* no me es posible el es-
cribirla por las ocupacio-
nes de las enpertinencias
q*ue* tray ConSigo estas *h*on-
ras y a Dios q*ue* otro Coreo
te escribire mas largo
*nuest*ro *señ*or te me *guard*e mas q*ue* a mi
*M*a*d*ri*d* y abril a 7 de *1688*
quien mas q*ue* a su bi-

da te quiere y desea ber
gelvira [rubrica]
[Hermano y Amigo mio ya mi mujer
Te dize la novedad de mi nuebo
Empleo y haviendo desseado
escrivirte mas largo no me
han dejado los embarazos en que me hallo
y el correo que Viene lo hare ponme
a los pies de mi hermana y a dios que te me guarde
tu hermano y Amigo
hasta morir
El Conde de Galve [rubrica]]

12. The Condesa de Galve to the Marqués del Cenete, Madrid,
24 April 1688, AL.

[fol. 1r]
querido de mi bida te aseguro me tienes Con el mayor Cuydado que es posible pues havien-
dote escrito no me has respon-
dido que nos han echado a mejico y no has hecho Caso y asi
te suplico me digas que ha sido
la causa que hasta berla estare çoçobrando en mis
himaginaciones por que en que
no me has querido faboreçer no
he de pensar y asi te pido
me saques de este Cuydado

y en el ynterin q*ue*dare pidi-
endo a Dios te me *guard*e mas q*ue* a mi
*Madri*d April 24 de *1*688
quien mas q*ue* a su bida
Te quiere y desea ber

13. The Condesa de Galve to the Marqués del Cenete, Cadiz, 4
July 1688, ALS.

[fol. 1]
q*ue*rido de mi bida y de mi Coraçon
no te podre decir Con la ternura
q*ue* tomo la pluma para despedir-
me de ti pues no sera ponderable
el sentimiento q*ue* me Cuesta
el acordarme q*ue* alego tanto de ti pues cuando tube el
gusto de q*ue* me escribiescas fue
Cuando no podia lograrlo
muy a menudo y asi te pido
no dejes de *h*açerlo sienpre q*ue*
hubiere forma q*ue* sera para mi
de gran gusto y te suplico me
encomiendes a dios q*ue*rido mio
nosotros trujimos un muy
buen bieage aunq*ue* yo muy des-
Consolada y manteniendome
asi todabia por q*ue* no se me qui-
tara *h*asta q*ue* logre lo q*ue* perdi
a mi hermana beso las m*ano*s y

[fol. 2]

q*ue* tenga *h*asta por suya por q*ue* la bre-
bedad del tienpo es mucho y yo
estoy muy mala de la Cabeça
q*ue*rido de mi bida Como no se
si te escribire otra no quiero dejar de decirte q*ue* de mis achaques antiguos aquellos q*ue* tu so-
lias gustar de saber en q*ue* estado
estaban se estan en el mismo
y asi no quiero sino q*ue* me Con-
sideres con medico nuebo y
fuera de madrid q*ue* desConsuelo llebara mi Coraçon y asi por
todo te pido me encomiendes a dios
a q*ue* te me *guard*e mas q*ue* a mi Cadiz
y Julio 4 de *1688*
quien mas q*ue* su bida
te quiere y desea ber
gelvira [rubrica]

14. The Condesa de Galve to the Marqués del Cenete, Mexico
City, 7 July 1689, LS.

[fol. 1r]
ex*celentisi*mo *señ*or
Hermano Y *señ*or mio El *señ*or Don Thomas
tello de Guzman es Sobrino del *señ*or
Don Andres tello (q*ue* este en Gloria) cavo
Gove*rnad*or de los Navios de Azogues q*ue* nos

conduxeron a este Reyno Y de quien
Rezivimos particulares atenziones
en todo nuestro biaje Y siendo este
cavallero de tan amables prendas que se ha savido Granxear la
voluntad de mi Primo quien haze
a vuestra excelencia particular Ynsinuazion para
que en las dependencias que tiene en
esa corte se sirva vuestra excelencia favorexerle
con toda Ynstanzia No puedo
negarme ha hazer a vuestra excelencia la supplica
[fol. 1v]
que baliere mi Ynterzession para que Don
Thomas consiga el entero cumplimiento
de su pretension Y siendo tanta la merzed
que devo a vuestra excelencia espero añadir esta
mas para que mi haixado experimen-
te por este medio lo que balen mis
Ynstanzias con vuestra excelencia cuya vida
guarde Dios muchos años Como deseo Y
he menester Mexico 7 de Jullio de 1689
Excelentisimo Señor
Besa las manos de Vuestra Excelencia su hermana
Gelvira la Condesa de Galve [rubrica]

Excelentisimo Señor Duque Duque Marques del Zenete mi
Señor Y mi hermano

15. The Condesa de Galve to the Marqués del Cenete, Mexico
City, 20 December 1689, LS.

[fol. 1r]

*Excelentisi*mo *señor*

Hermano y Señor mio de singular
esttimacion *h*a sido para mi la con
q*ue vuestra excelencia* me favoreçe de 12 de Junio
Solizitando las noticias de mi salud
que es feliz desde que llegue a este
Reino pues no me han repetido los
continuos accidentes que padezia en
esa cortte y ssi le mereciere a *vuestra* e*xcelenci*a
repetidas hordenes de su Servizio
se me añadira el gusto de obedezerlas
al desseo que le manifiesta mi
voluntad y estimo a *vuestra excelencia* como es de
mi obligacion la en*h*orabuena que se
sirve darme del nuebo Sobrino
hijo de mi Hermano el Marques de Tabara que ha sido nueba
para mi muy Conforme a mi desseo
*vuestra excelenci*a me tiene con ttodo afecto
para quanto fuere de su maior
agrado guarde Dios

[fol. 1v]

a V*uestra* e*xcelenci*a hermano y señor mio
quanto puede y he menester Me-
xico 20 de Diziembre de 1689

[^ *Excelentisi*mo *Seño*r

Besa las *m*a*n*os de *vuestra excelencia* su
her*m*a*n*a y *m*e*n*or ser*vi*do*r*a

Appendix 4

Gelvira la Condesa de galve [rubrica]]

E*xcelentisi*mo *señor* Duque Du*que* Mar*que*s del cenete mi her-
m*a*no y *señor*/

16. The Condesa de Galve to the Marqués del Cenete, Mexico
City, 28 January 1690, LS.

[fol. 1r]
E*xelentisi*mos *señor*
Hermano y *señor* mio por Cartta de 30 de Junio
del año pasado de 1689 me hordena V*uestra* e*xcelencia* asista
a dos Religiosos de la horden de n*ues*tro Padre
San Fran*zis*co que pasaron a estte Reyno a pedir
limosnas para la Canonizacion de S*a*n Pedro de
Regalados y attendiendo a ser mandato de
V*uestra* e*xcelencia* demas de ser obra de tanta piedad p*ue*de
estar v*uestra* e*xcelencia* ciertto que enquanto pudiere contribui-
re de mi partte a que los Religiosos Consigan
se adelante la limosna quanto fuere posible
fomenttando a estte fin los animos (aunque son
tanttas las necesidades que ocurren de diferen-
tes Santuarios y Ymajenes que los tienen Vien
corttos) para que Cohoperen y acudan con las
suyas pues redunda en tantto servicio de
Dios *h*asta a*h*ora no me han Visto estos
religiosos pero crea V*uestra* E*xcelencia* los Solicitare para
ayudarles en quantto p*ue*da y deseo tener muchos
[fol. 1v]
motivos del agrado y servicio de V*uestra* e*xcelencia* en q*ue*

experimentte mi Volunttad y buen afectto
Nuestro señor guarde la excelentisima perssona de Vuestra
excelencia los muchos/
años que he menester Mejico 28 de Henero de 1690
[^Excelentsimo señor
Besa la mano de vuestra excelencia su hermana
y menor serbidora
Gelvira la Condesa de galve [rubrica]]

Excelentisimo señor Duque Duque Marques del Cenette mi
Hermano y señor

17. The Condesa de Galve to the Marqués del Cenete, Mexico
City, 2 February 1690, LS.

[fol. 1r]
Excelentsimo señor
Hermano Y señor mio bien save vuestra excelencia que
Ysavel Solano me sirvio con buena ley
y cariño hastta que se caso en chamartin Ha me
escriptto ahora sintiendo mi ausencia y significando-
me algunas descomodidades porque su marido aunque es hombre de vien no ttiene ocupacion en que
ejercittarse para ganar para su alimentto y
haviendola yo querido vien y deseandola
su alivio y el reparo de sus descomodidades
no puedo dejar de Suplicar a vuestra excelencia se
sirva de hacerme merced de favoreserla
y a su Marido acomodandole en alguna cossa
la que a vuestra excelencia le pareciere para que gane

la comida q*ue* se lo estimare a *vuestra excelencia*
teniendole por mi recomendado para quanto
se le ofreciere porq*ue* aseguro a *vuestra excelencia*
quiero vien a Ysavel por el especial afectto
con q*ue* me sirvio y espero q*ue* estto
[fol. 1v]
sea vastantte para q*ue* *vuestra excelencia* no la olvide
y q*ue* me dispense muchas ocasiones de su
agrado en q*ue* Servir a *vuestra excelencia* cuya e*x*celentisima
perss*on*a Gua*r*de Dios los m*u*c*h*os años q*ue* deseo Mejico
2 de febre*r*o de 1690
[^E*x*c*el*entis*im*o señor
besa las m*an*os de *vuestra excelenci*a su herm*an*a
y m*en*or serbidora
*Gelvi*ra la Condesa de Galve [rubrica]]

E*x*c*el*entisi*m*o se*ñ*or Duque Duque Marq*ue*s del cenete
Herm*an*o y se*ñ*or/

18. The Condesa de Galve to the Marqués del Cenete, Mexico
City, 21 August 1692, LS

[fol. 1r]
E*x*c*el*ents*im*o se*ñ*or
Hermano y se*ñ*or mio haviendo tenido por
Carta de Don Juan de Montufar que en-
camino por irregulares vias y llego
en mayo de este año a manos de mi
Primo la noticia de que su Mage*sta*d (Di-
os le *guar*de) hizo a *Vuestra Excelenci*a del Conss*e*jo de

estado siendo mi obligacion el dar
a Vuestra Excelencia la henhorabuena me valgo del
medio de esta manifestando me ha
sido de singular alvorozo este avi-
so y le puedo asegurar a Vuestra excelencia con
verdad fue menester para tolerar
la desazon que se padeze en esta
tierra y la soledad con que se
vive añadiendose la gran pesadum-
bre y susto que tuve el dia ocho
de Junio con el tulmulto de los
[fol. 1v]
Yndios cuyo contratiempo me tuvo con
gran sinsavor y mas quando tenia
tan en el riesgo a mi Primo a qui-
en se deve tener gran lastima pues
no le vale para experimentar esto
su buena intencion zelo y desinte-
res en el servicio de su Magestad (que
Dios guarde) ni tampoco lo mucho que
siendo solo ha hecho previniendo lo
sucedido ya gracias a nuestro señor se conti-
nua el sosiego y le tuvo desde el
otro dia con las prevenciones y
reparos que puso Vuestra Excelencia me tiene a
su disposicion devajo de cuyo seguro
puede mandarme con el de que sera obe-
decido Dios guarde la Excelentisima persona de Vuestra
excelencia
mi señor y mi Hermano los muchos años que pue-

de Mexico 21 de Agosto de 1692
[^Excelentisimo señor
Besa las manos de Vuestra Excelencia su hermana
y mas segura servidora
Gelvira la Condesa de Galve [rubrica]]

Excelentisimo Señor Duque Duque Marques del Zenete mi
señor y mi Hermano/

19. The Condesa de Galve to the Marqués del Cenete, Mexico
City, January 1693, LS.

[fol. 1r]
Excelentisimo Señor
Hermano Y señor mio Doy Respuesta a Dos
de vuestra excelencia sus fechas de 14 de Jullio del año
de 1691 Y otra de 20 de Junio del año
passado dexandome muy gustossa las no-
ticias que vuestra excelencia se sirbe darme de mantener-
sse en cabal salud que Ruego a nuestro señor sea
por muchos a:os pudiendo dezir a vuestra excelencia de
la mia es bien mala pues quedo padezien-
do del accidente antiguo que me maltrata
lo bastante pero de qualquier suerte para
serbir a vuestra excelencia deseandome de muchas ocasiones de su agrado Y que nuestro señor guarde a vuestra
excelencia/
muchos años como deseo Mexico Y enero de
1693
[^Excelentsimo Señor

Besa las ma*nos* de V*uestra Excelencia* Su
her*ma*na y m*e*nor Ser*vidor*a
Gelvira la Condessa de Galve [rubrica]]

E*xcelentisi*mo Se*ño*r Duque Duque Marques del zenet*e* mi
her*ma*no Y se*ñor*/

20. The Condesa de Galve to the Duquesa del Infantado,
Mexico City, 20 January 1693, L and ALS.

[fol. 1r]
E*xcelentisi*ma se*ño*ra
Mi se*ño*ra Y mi herm*a*na Y Amiga de mi vida con el
avisso Y flota qu*e* arribaron a estos Reinos *h*e
rezibido tres tuias sus *fec*has de 16-17 Y 26 de
Junio del año passado dexandome la ultima
con el cuidado que debes considerar por lo que
me dizes de *h*averte buelto a sobrebenir el accidente de las tercianas sencillas que ruego
a n*uest*ro se*ño*r te halles ia tan mexorada Como mi
cariño te desea i que mi herm*a*no Y demas sobrinos gozen de muy perfecta salud que te aseguro me da bastante cuidado el ber lo que mi
herm*a*no trabaxa no ocasionandome lo menos
mi Primo (que se pone a tus pies) pues aqui *h*ai
el bastante Y *h*aver padezido mucho de falta de
salud de que ia gloria a Dios queda muy me-
jorado que no es poco con los cuidados i pessadumbres que *h*a tenido de que ia se avisso a essa

corte con el antecedente que a este Salio Para
essos Reinos io quedo bien mala por *h*averme
buelto a repetir el accidente que en essa corte Y aqui *h*e padezido i me *h*a obligado a San-
grar dos bezes de que aunque quedo mejor
Siempre con el rezelo de si me bolbera
[fol. 1v]
Mucho te estimo el regalo que recibi por
mano de Benito de Cartajena que todo es muy
como de tu mano i en que no escusso dezirte se co-
noze mal la falta de comerzio con francia in-
galaterra pero en tus primores todo cabe io
quedo muy engreida con el Y con la justa esti-
mazion que debo Y me *h*e alegrado mucho con la
noticia que me das de *h*aversse buelto a essa corte
mis sobrinos los de Lemos para que tu tengas
el contento de tenerlos cerca Y pues sabes quanto deseo el serbirte no escusses el mandarme que
io Reserbo para de buelta de flota el escribirte mas largo i te remitire el produzido de lo
que bino en las gabarras de azogues en la for-
ma que me lo mandas *nuest*ro *señ*or te *guar*de mi *señ*ora Y mi
herm*a*na los muchos años q*ue* deseo en compa:ia de mi
herm*a*n*o* cuias m*ano*s Besso Mex*i*co Y enero 20
de 1693
[^Mi *señ*ora y mi *h*ermana bien
Creras de mi Cariño Con
Cuanta mortificacion
me tiene tu poca Salud
pues Solo las q*ue* lo espri-

mentamos Sabemos el
trabajo que espero ya espero
[fol. 2r]
en dios ya habras Conba-
lecido enteramente pues
eso es lo que yo no Se haçer
que en estando mejor es
Cuando Caygo Con mas
fuerça dios me de paci-
encia y tanbien me la
de para la ynpaciencia
que tengo de no haberte podido remitir aquella mine-
ria que pareçe algo seguro
Se resiste de llegar por alla
yo me holgare de que quedes
Con la Satisfacion de que te
desseo Serbir que en la flota yra y te escribire
Excelentisima señora
Te besa las manos tu hermana
y amiga
Gelvira [rubrica]]

excelentisima señora Duquessa del Ynfantado mi señora mi
hermana Y Amiga /

21. The Condesa de Galve to the Marqués de Távara, Mexico
City, 28 May 1693, L and ALS.

Appendix 4

[fol. 1r]
Herm*a*no y querido mio de mi vida teniendo la
ocasion de esta flota que buelbe a hazer su torna-
biaje no *h*e querido dexar de escrivirte estos renglones para significarte por medio de ellos de quanto gusto sera para mi el saber te mantienes en
cabal salud acompanada con la de mi herm*a*na i
demas sobrinos i que esta se continue por los muchos a:os que deseo io quedo para serbirte
sin poder arribar de mis continuos achaques pues para ello aiudan poco los gustos que aqui *h*ay
pues las pessadumbres de estos dias passados *h*an sido
bien grandes de que ia tendras noticia por la que te
escrivi en el avisso passado i a*h*ora lo que siento es
el que nuestra buelta a essos reinos no sea en esta
ocassion i solo me consuela la esperanza de que sera en la que biene que te aseguro lo deseo mucho pues
es aqui no *h*ay forma de poder arribar ni recuperar
mi salud mi Primo gloria a Dios se halla mas
combalezi*e*nte que tambien *h*a padezido bastante quiebra en la suia i te B*esa las* m*a*nos i io te pido que pues sabes soy muy tuia no escusses el mandarme quan-
to sea de tu agrado n*uest*ro se*ñ*or te *gua*rde herm*a*no Y querido
mio
los m*ucho*s años que deseo Mex*i*co Y Maio 28 de 1693
[^E mi q*u*erido por aca no *h*ay q*ue* poderte escribir Sino q*ue* estos penos
[fol. 1v]
q*ue*dan quietos eso Con la des-
Confianca q*ue* mere*ç*e lo q*ue* bi-

mos y Supuesto q*ue* desde q*ue*
bine no he escrito mas q*ue*
lamentaciones no he de salir esta bez de lo mismo
y Con mas raçon pues a mi
Cada dia se me agraba mas
mis achaqu*es* q*ue* te aseguro estoy bieja y Consumida pero
Con esperancas de q*ue* en yendo
por alla me recobrare mi
primo esta mejor aunq*ue* Cada dia gomitando y dan-
dole Susbaydos q*ue* me tien*e*
Con *h*arto Cuydado y asi tu
q*ue* estas sin ellos escribeme
muy largo q*ue* es el gusto q*ue* aqui
puedo tener y a dios q*ue* te g*uar*de
Tuya mas alla de morir
aunq*ue* no quieras
Gelvira [rubrica]]

El Marques de Tavara mi herm*an*o y *seño*r

22. The Condesa de Galve to the Duquesa del Infantado y Pastrana, Marquesa del Cenete, Mexico City, 28 May 1693, L and ALS.

[fol. 1r]
*Ex*c*elentisi*ma *seño*ra
Mi *seño*ra mi herm*an*a Y Amiga de mi Vida en el avisso

passado te escrivi i a*h*ora lo repito por el Sumo gusto que en ello tengo i tambien por lo que deseo tener noticias de tu Salud q*ue* me alegarare Sea
tan Cumplida Como io deseo i que Çuzeda lo mismo
a mi herm*an*o i demas sobrinos cuias manos besso i mi
Primo se pone a tus pies i io quedo para serbirte en
todo aunque bien mala pues la repeticion de mis accidentes me tiene tan maltratada la Caveza que no
me da lugar a escrivir de mi mano i assi me Supli-
ras el que baia de la ajena i a*h*ora passo a dezirte Como
remito el dinero Segun me tienes ordenado a Poder
de D*o*n Pablo Bizarron en quien lo *h*allaras quando
gustares embiar por el que io quedare muy gustossa
en *h*averte azertado a Serbir Como tambien lo hago en lo
que me dizes de que no te embie Cossa que
Se quiebre por lo qual no ban Barros que Solo te remito una Ymajen de Guadalupe por estar tocada
al orijinal i ser tu tan debota de la Señor i esse
chocolate que me alegrare Salga a tu gusto para
que Con esso no eches menos el no ser muy buenos
los abanicos que te embio pues como este año
*h*a faltado la nao de China no se *h*a *h*allado Cossa
de probecho i assi perdonaras la Cortedad del regalo que para quando io baia procurare llebar de
[fol. 1v]
los mejores que ia deseo llegue el dia de que nos
beamos en essa Corte i en el interin no escusses
el mandarme pues Sabes Soy muy tuia n*ues*tro *señor* te
*gua*rde mi *señ*ora Y mi herm*an*a los muchos años que deseo/
Mexico Y Maio 28 de 1693

[^Mi querida ay ba la memoria
de las rifas por si gustares de entretenerte en leer-
la y que sepas que soy mujer de
cuenta y racon el dinero que
recaba enpleado en Cacao
para que Don Pablo biçaron lo
venda y te enbie la Cuenta
que por ser el Corespondiente
de mi primo y muy honbre
de bien se lo he remitido a el
diciendo que obedezca lo que tu
le mandaras me holgare que
desgustosa con esta disposicion pues mi desseo es ese
yo estoy como Sienpre y por a-
ca no hay nobedad que todo esta quieto/
[^Excelentisima señora te besa las manos tu hermana
y mas segura amiga
Gelvira [rubrica]]
Excelentisima señora Duquessa del Infantado y de Pastrana mi
señora/
Excelentisima señora Duquessa Duquessa Marquessa
del Zenette mi señora mi hermana Y Amiga/
[fol. 2r]
Memoria de las piezas de christal que se remitie-
ron para Venderse Con los prezios que por la tasa mas
alta se podian dar por ellas que sirvio de luz para ri-
farse aunque con Variedad

Una copita labrada guarnezida con
Un esmaltico rojo y berde tasada en o-
chenta pesos   0080
Otra como taza con Una guarnizionzi-
ta al principio del pie tasada en setenta
y quatro pesos   0074
Una escudilla de christal lisa guarne-
zida con Un pie dorado y asas tasada
en sesenta Y quatro pesos   0064
Un Cubiletico sin guarnizion ninguna
labrado tasado en ziento Y veinte pesos   0120
                                                0338

[fol. 2v]
Vienen de la buelta trezientos y treinta
y ocho pesos   0338
Otro Cubilete con tapador y asas con una
guarnizionzica tasado en zien pesos   0100
Una copa en canos de carmona con su pie
tasada en dozientos pesos   0200
Un aguamanil con el asa y pie de oro Y
Unos asientos de perlas y rubies tasado en
zien pesos   0100
Un pomico redondo con su boquita de oro
esmaltada de negro tasado en doze pesos   0012
otro pomito mas chato de christal tasado
en diez pesos   0010
Otra cuba de christal sin tapadera ta-
sada en diez pesos   0010
otra cubita de christal con su tapaderita
al lado tasada en diez pesos   0010

[fol. 3r]

Vienen de la buelta setezientos y ochenta	0780
tres urnitas de christal sin guarnizer ta-	
sadas en Veinte Y quatro pesos cada Una	
Valen setenta Y dos pesos	0072
Una caja de christal redonda y chata	
Guarnezida tasada en catorce pesos	0014
Una caxa de christal larga guarnezida	
tasada en doze pesos	0012
dentro de dicha caja otra de christal chi-	
quita labrada con Unos muellezitos que tie-	
nen quatro turquesas y esmaltados de negro	
tasada en veinte Y seis pesos	026
Otra Caja en forma de Corazon de christal	
guarnezida tasada en diez y seis pesos	0016
Una casta:a de christal pequeña tasa-	
da en doze pesos	0012
dos cubitas de christal chiquitas con sus	
espitas tasadas en Veinte pesos	0020
	0952

[fol. 3v]

Vienen de la buelta novezientos y zinquenta	
y dos	0952
Una bola de christal tasada en catorze pesos	0014
Una caja de christal azul guarnezida tasa-	
da en diez pesos	0010
Una tarjeta de christal aobada con almeni-	
llas en que esta pintado un san antonio tasada	
en quarenta pesos	0040
Unas arracadas en forma de aguilas con unos	

rubies tasadas en dozientos y setenta pesos	0260
otra caja de christal en forma de estrella tasada	
en diez y seis pesos	0016
Una cuba de Venturina con su espita tasa-	
da en ocho pesos	0008
Una arquita de Venturina chiquita con	
sus muellezicos de feligrana tasada en diez pesos	0010
Una Cubita chiquita de Venturina	
Con su espita guarnezida de esmalte azul	
y dos cadenitas tasada en Veinte pesos	0020
	1U330

Importan (como parece) las piezas de Christal
y Venturina mil tresientos y treinta pesos segun la
tassa Y lo procedido de las Rifas fueron mil qua-
trocientos y sesenta y nueve con que se aumento la
[fol. 4r]
Cantidad de ciento y treinta y nueve pesos sobre
la tassa ettcetera

Lo sacado de las Rifas	1U469 pesos
La tassa	1U330 pesos
El aumento	U139 pesos

23. The Condesa de Galve to the Marqués del Cenete, Mexico
City, 4 June 1693, LS.

[fol. 1r]
*Excelentisi*mo se*ñ*or
Herm*a*no Y se*ñ*or mio aunq*ue* en el avisso passado
escrivi a V*uestra Excelencia* lo repito ahora por solicitar no-

ticias de la salud de *Vuestra Excelencia* que me alegrare sea tan
cumplida como deseo i q*ue* goze de este beneficio
mi herm*a*na Y demas sobrinos cuias manos besso
yo q*ue*do para serbir a *Vuestra Excelencia* algo mas mejorada de mi poca salud aunque no del todo pero me
sirbe de consuelo el ber a mi primo quan alentado
se *h*alla que tambien *h*a padezido bastante quiebra en
la suia que no es poco el que haia podido arribar
con el continuo trabajo que tiene i bea *Vuestra Excelencia* si le
puedo serbir en algo que lo hare con mucho gusto
n*ue*stro s*e*ñor guar*d*e a *Vuestra Excelencia* los m*uch*os años
que deseo Mex*i*co
Y Junio 4 de 1693
[^Excelentisimo s*e*ñor
*B*es*a l*as *m*anos de v*uestra excelencia* su
her*m*ana y *m*en*o*r ser*vid*or*a*
*Gel*v*ira* la Condesa de Galve [rubrica]]

*Excelentis*imo s*e*ñor Duque Duque Marques del Zenet*e* mi
her*m*ano y s*e*ñor

24. The Condesa de Galve to the Duque del Infantado y
Pastrana, Marqués del Cenete, Mexico City, 28 June 1693, LS.

[fol. 1r]
*Excelentis*imo s*e*ñor
Herm*a*no Y s*e*ñor mio Con el avisso q*ue* acaba de
llegar de essos a estos Reinos he recibido dos
de *V*uestra Excelencia Y la ultima de *f*echa de 11 de febrero passado en que podra *V*uestra Excelencia conozer de mi b*u*en

afecto i cariño que professaba a mi hermana (que
Sancta gloria haia) de quanto sentimiento me
havra sido su falta de que doy a Vuestra Excelencia el pessa-
me asegurandole le acompa:o Con las maiores
beras en Semejante dolor el qual solo me le podra alibiar el saber que Vuestra Excelencia goze de muy
cumplida salud que pido a nuestro señor sea por muchos años io quedo para serbir a Vuestra Excelencia algo
mas mejorada y deseando que nuestro señor le guarde los
muchos años que puede Mexico Y Junio 28 de 1693
[^Excelentisimo señor
Besa los manos de Vuestra Excelencia su hermana
y menor servidora
Gelvira la Condesa de Galve [rubrica]]

Excelentisimo señor Duque Duque Marques del Zenete mi
hermano Y señor/

25. The Condesa de Galve to don Manrique de Silva y
Mendoza, Mexico City, 25 June 1694, LS.

[fol. 1r]
Sobrino y señor mio Haviendo tenido no-
tizia del fallecimiento de mi hermano el señor
Duque del Imfantado (que haya gloria) no
permite mi obligacion deje de concurrir a cumplir con ella dando a vuestra señoria el pesame de
esta perdida en que he sido tan interesada
porque acompaño a vuestra señoria con las mayores
veras en el Justo sentimiento que le habra

ocassionado Desseando que n*uest*ro *señor* con-
zeda a V*uestra Señoria* muy dilatada salud y le *guarde*
muchos y felizes años Mexico y Junio
25 de 1694
[^B*esa* l*as* m*an*os de v*uestra señoria* su tia
y m*en*or ser*vidor*a
Gelvira la Condesa de Galve [rubrica]]

señor Don Man*ue*l de silva y Mendosa mi sobrino y *señor*

26. The Condesa de Galve to the Marqués de Távara, Mexico
City, 26 June 1694, LS and ALS.

[fol. 1r]
Hermano y *señor* mio No permite mi cariño
pierda la ocassion de escrivirte en *e*ste aviso
que se despacha a esos Reynos quedando mor-
tificada de lo mucho que se han rretardado
las notizias de ellos pues *h*a un año que nos
hallamos sin ellas y Yo sin las tuyas mucho
mas por haver dexado de escrivir en todas
las ocassiones atribuyolo a descuydo de no
havertelas avissado de Madrid devien-
dome el que considere tu cariño por el mio
pues quien vien quiere tarde olvida me holgare gozes muy cumplida salud en comp*añi*a
de mi hermana y que te *h*aya conzedido n*uest*ro
señor Dilatada subzession con las felizidades q*ue*
mi verdadero afecto y voluntad te previene
que seran bien cumplidas yo quedo con bien

poca salud padeziendo estos dias considerable
quiebra por haverme sobrevenido unas pos-
temas q*ue* me han abierto en parte muy delica-
da que me han tenido mas de un mes en
[fol. 1v]
la cama padeziendo grandes dolores a*h*ora
quedo lebantada y mexor (a Dios grazias)
aunque todavia *e*sta la llaga abierta con
que puedes considerarme lo violenta que estare en *e*ste rreyno sobre el poco gusto que yo tenia *h*Arto desseo que este año benga subzesor
a mi Primo para que nos podamos bolver quanto
antes de que tengo vivas esperanzas por lograr el berte que es mi unico an*h*elo quiers
n*uest*ro s*e*ñor conzedermelo Aqui no *h*ay nobedad
particular de que avisarte suplicote no dejes de escrivirme en todas las ocass*i*ones que *h*ubie-
re dandome este gusto y el de avisarme lo
que te se ofreziere de tu agrado pues saves
con el cariño y voluntad que en todo te
obedezere Dios te g*uar*de m*uch*os años como desseo
y he m*ene*ster Mex*i*co y Junio 26 de 1694
[^mi q*ue*rido mi poca Salud no
me da lugar a escribirte de
mi mano y muy largo
t*r*ata de *h*açerlo tu para de-
senogarme
te besa las m*a*nos tu herm*a*na
q*ue* mas te quiere y desea ber
Gelvira [rubrica]]

Hermano y *señor* Marques de tavara

27. The Condesa de Galve to the Marqués de Távara, Mexico City, 5 June 1696, ALS.

[fol. 1r]
hermano y querido de mi bida
y de mi coraçon con la ocasion
de despachar mi primo este
abiso te digo cuan alboroçada
estoy de haber recibido dos cartas
tuyas la mas fresca de 28 de Junio
que en estando tu bueno lo de demas ynporta menos harto siento el que todabia te estes meti-
do por esos rincones pero espero en dios que todos hemos de
sacar la cabeça a un tienpo pues
ha sido dios serbido de que nosotros nos bemos en esta flota
que te aseguro estoy loca de contento y aunque el camino es tan
penoso y tan peligroso no le tengo miedo sino es deseo de
poner me en el Creo que sera
nuestra salida de aqui a pri-
meras de mayo y de la veracruz a mediado de Junio con
[fol. 1v]

que espero en dios el q*ue* nos
*h*emos de ber este año y por eso
no te pienso escribir muy largo q*ue* estamos muy de priesa
asi para despachar este abiso
como para las prebenciones de
nuestra jornada nos bere-
mos y *h*ablaremos de nuebe
años q*ue* aq*ui* no nos bemos y he lo
te quiero decir q*ue ha* sido grande lastima la muerte de bri-
gida q*ue* se caso y no a mi gusto
y pario una muchacha y se
murio del parto con q*ue* yo la
tengo en casa dandome mu-
cho en q*ue* entender porq*ue* no
tiene mas q*ue* un año y la *h*e de llebar mamando ella es fea cu-
anto puede sea pero muy bu-
fona por aca no *h*ay nobeda-
des de q*ue* poderte abisar y si
*hu*viere algunas sera cuando mi primo dege el gobierno esas las llebare yo *h*acia
alla pero lo q*ue* no llebare
[fol. 2r]
seran criadas pues *h*ay gran
priesa a casarse se caso una
muger moca q*ue* tu no conoces
y una de la camara y a*h*ora

esta para casarse otras dos
y una es do:a manuela y
*h*arto lo siento porq*ue* se queda
por aca y en biendonos *h*ablaremos muchas cosas y pide-
le a dios q*ue* lo logremos y su m*agesta*d
te me *guar*de mi q*ue*rido de mi bida
como he m*enes*ter Mexico y Junio a 5
de *1696*
quien mas te quiere y es
tuya *h*asta morir
Gelvira [rubrica]

BIBLIOGRAPHY

WORKS CITED

Archival Materials

Archivo General de Indias, Seville, Spain
    Contratación 5450:47
    México 610

Archivo General de Notarías del Distrito Federal, Mexico City,
    Sección Histórica 692 (1696)

Archivo Histórico Nacional, Madrid, Spain
    Sección Osuna, Cartas

Archivo Histórico de Protocolos de Madrid, Spain
    P. 10.890; P. 12.118

Church of Jesus Christ of Latter-day Saints Genealogical
Collection
    Sagrario Metropolitano, Lista de miembros (1695), microfilm
0036415

Other Works

Anes, Gonzalo. "La 'Depresión' agraria durante el siglo xvii en
Castilla." In *Homenaje a Julio Caro Baroja*. Eds. Antonio Carreira,

Jesús Antonio Cid, Manuel Gutiérrez Esteve, and Rogelio Rubio. Madrid: Centro de Investigaciones Sociológicas, 1978.

Arcila Farías, Eduardo. *Comercio entre Venezuela y México en los siglos xvi y xvii.* Mexico City: Colegio de México, 1950.

Arenal, Electa, and Stacey Schlau. *Untold Sisters: Hispanic Nuns in Their Own Works.* Trans. Amanda Powell. Albuquerque: Univ. of New Mexico Press, 1989.

Arteaga y Falguera, Cristina. *La Casa del Infantado, cabeza de los Mendoza.* 2 vols. Madrid: El Duque del Infantado, 1944.

Astete, Gaspar de. *Del govierno de la familia y estado de las viudas y donzellas. Dirigido a doña María de Acuña, Condessa de Buendía.* Burgos: En la imprenta de Philipe de Junta, por Juan Baptista Varesio, 1597.

———. *Del govierno de la familia, y estado del matrimonio: Donde se trata, de como se han de aver los casados con sus mugeres, y los padres con sus hijos, y los señores con sus criados. Dirigido a don Martín Manrique de Padilla y Acuña, adelantado mayor de Castilla, Conde de Sancta Gadea, y capitan general de las galeras y armada de España.* Valladolid: Por Alonso de Vega, 1598.

Barrionuevo, Jerónimo de. *Avisos.* 2 vols. Madrid: Ediciones Atlas, 1969.

Bataillon, Marcel. *Erasmo y España: Estudios sobre la historia espiritual del siglo xvi.* Sección de Obras de Historia. Trans. Antonio Alatorre. 2d ed. Mexico City: Fondo de Cultura Económica, 1966.

Bellini, Giuseppe. *Sor Juana e i suoi misteri: Studio e testi.* Milan:

BIBLIOGRAPHY

Cisalpino-Goliardica, 1987.

Bolton, Herbert Eugene. *Rim of Christendom: A Biography of Eusebio Francisco Kino, Pacific Coast Pioneer.* 1936. Rpt. Tucson: The Univ. of Arizona Press, 1984.

Braudel, Fernand. *Capitalism and Material Life, 1400–1800.* Trans. Miriam Kochan. New York: Harper Torchbooks, Harper and Row, 1975.

Brown, Jonathan, and J.H. Elliott. *A Palace for a King: The Buen Retiro and the Court of Philip IV.* New Haven: Yale Univ. Press, 1980.

Callejo, Carlos. *El Monasterio de Guadalupe.* Los Monumentos Cardinales de España, 21. Madrid: Editorial Plus-Ultra, 1958.

Cavo, Andrés. *Historia de México.* Ed. Ernest J. Burrus. Mexico City: Editorial Patria, 1949.

Chandler, Richard E., and Kessel Schwartz. *A New History of Spanish Literature.* Baton Rouge: Louisiana State Univ. Press, 1961.

Cossío, José María de. *Los toros: Tratado técnico e histórico.* Madrid: Espasa-Calpe, 1947.

Crosby, James O. *En torno a la poesía de Quevedo.* Madrid: Editorial Castalia, 1967.

Cruickshank, W. "'Literature' and the Book Trade in Golden-Age Spain." *The Modern Language Review* 73 (Oct. 1978).

Cruz, Sor Juana Inés de la. *Los empeños de una casa.* Colección

Ediciones y Estudios. Ed. Celsa Carmen García Valdés. Barcelona: Promociones y Publicaciones S.A., 1989.

Cunqueiro, Alvaro. *A cociña galega*. Vigo: Editorial Galaxia, 1973.

Davies, R. Trevor. *Spain in Decline, 1621–1700*. London: Macmillan & Co., 1957.

Delieto y Peñuela, José. *La mala vida en la España de Felipe IV.* 2d ed. Madrid: Espasa-Calpe, 1951.

———. *La mujer, la casa y la moda (en la España del rey poeta)*. 2d ed. Madrid: Espasa-Calpe, 1954.

Diccionario de Autoridades. Biblioteca Románica Hispánica. 3 vols. 1726–37. Facs. ed. Madrid: Editoral Gredos, 1979.

Diccionario Porrúa de historia, biografía y geografía de México. 2 vols. Mexico City: Editorial Porrúa, 1964, 1976.

Domínguez Ortiz, Antonio. *El antiguo régimen: Los Reyes Católicos y los Austria*. Vol. 3 of *Historia de España Alfaguara*. Ed. Miguel Artola. Madrid: Ediciones Alfaguara, 1973.

———."La crisis en Castilla en 1677–1687." In *Historia económica de España*. Ed. Juan Hernández Andreu. Madrid: Confederación Española de Cajas de Ahorros, 1978.

———. *Las clases privilegiadas en la España del Antiguo Régimen*. Colección Fundamentos, 31. Madrid: Ediciones ISTMO, 1975.

———. "Los gastos de corte en la España del siglo xvii." In *Homenaje a Jaime Vicens Vives*. Ed. J. Maluquer de Motes. 2 vols.

Barcelona: Universidad de Barcelona, Facultad de Filosofía y Letras, 1967.

———. "Un virreinato en venta." *Mercurio Peruano* 49 (En.-Feb. 1965).

Elliott, J.H. *The Count-Duke of Olivares: The Statesman in an Age of Decline.* New Haven: Yale Univ. Press, 1986.

———. *Imperial Spain: 1469–1716.* New York: New American Library, 1966.

———."Foreign Policy and Domestic Crisis: Spain, 1598–1659." In J.H. Elliott. *Spain and Its World, 1500–1700: Selected Essays.* New Haven: Yale Univ. Press, 1989.

———. "Poder y propaganda en la España de Felipe IV." In *Homenaje a José Antonio Maravall.* Eds. María Carmen Iglesias, Carlos Moya, and Luis Rodríguez Zúñiga. 3 vols. Madrid: Centro de Investigaciones Sociológicas, 1985.

———. "The Spanish Peninsula 1598–1648." In *The Decline of Spain and the Thirty Years War, 1609–48/59.* Ed. J.P. Cooper. Vol. 4 of *The New Cambridge Modern History.* Cambridge: Cambridge Univ. Press, 1970.

Escriche, Joaquín. *Diccionario razonado de legislación y jurisprudencia.* 4 vols. 1888. Rpt. Bogotá: Editorial Temis, 1977.

Espinosa, J. Manuel. "The Virgin of the Reconquest of New Mexico." *Mid-America: An Historical Review* 18 (Apr. 1936).

Farfán, Fray Agustín. *Tractado breve de medicina.* 1592. Facs. ed.

Madrid: Ediciones Cultura Hispánica, 1944.

Fayard, Janine. *Les membres du Conseil de Castille a l'époque moderne, 1621–1746.* Geneva: Droz, 1979.

Fernández Alvarez, Manuel. *La sociedad española en el siglo de oro.* 2d ed. 2 vols. Madrid: Editorial Gredos, 1989.

———— et al. "La demografía de Salamanca en el siglo xvi a través de los fondos parroquiales." In *Homenaje al Dr. d. Juan Reglà Campistol.* 2 vols. Valencia: Facultad de Filosofía y Letras, Univ. de Valencia, 1975.

Fernández de Béthencourt, Francisco. *Historia genealógica y heráldica de la monarquía española, casa real y grandes de España.* 10 vols. Madrid: E. Teodoro, 1912.

Ferry, Robert J. *The Colonial Elite of Early Caracas: Formation and Crisis, 1567–1767.* Berkeley: Univ. of California Press, 1989.

Gage, Thomas. *Thomas Gage's Travels in the New World.* Norman: Univ. of Oklahoma Press, 1958.

García, Genaro. *Tumultos y rebeliones acaecidos en México.* Vol. 10 of *Documentos inéditos o muy raros para la historia de México.* Mexico City: Secretaría de la Reforma Agraria, 1981.

García Carraffa, Alberto, and Arturo García Carraffa. *Diccionario heráldico y genealógico de apellidos españoles y americanos.* 88 vols. Madrid: Nueva Imprenta Radio, 1943.

García Payón, José. *Amaxocoatl o libro del chocolate.* Toluca: Tip. Escuela de Artes, 1936.

Gemelli Careri, Giovanni Francesco. *Viaje a la Nueva España*. Trans. José María de Agreda y Sánchez. 2 vols. Mexico City: Jorge Porrúa, 1983.

Gibson, Charles. *The Aztecs Under Spanish Rule: A History of the Indians of the Valley of Mexico, 1519–1810*. Stanford: Stanford Univ. Press, 1964.

Gómez-Centurión Jiménez, Carlos. "La familia, la mujer y el niño." In *La vida cotidiana en la España de Velázquez*. Ed. José D. Alcalá-Zamora. Colección Historia, 4. Madrid: Ediciones Temas de Hoy, 1989.

Granjel, Luis S. *La medicina española del siglo xvii*. Salamanca: Ediciones Univ. de Salamanca, 1978.

Gutiérrez Coronel, Diego. *Historia genealógica de la Casa de Mendoza*. Biblioteca Conquense, 3. Cuenca: Instituto Jerónimo Zurita del Consejo Superior de Investigaciones Científicas, 1946.

Haring, C.H. *The Spanish Empire in America*. 1943. Rpt. New York: Harcourt, Brace and World, Inc., Harbinger Books, 1963.

Hermosilla Molina, Antonio. *Cien años de medicina sevillana: La regia sociedad de medicina y demás ciencias, de Sevilla, en el siglo xviii*. Historia, 3. Seville: La Excelentísima Diputación Provincial de Sevilla, 1970.

Huarte de San Juan, Juan. *Examen de ingenios: The Examination of mens wits. In which, by discovering the varietie of natures, is shewed for what profession each one is apt, and how far he shall profit therein.*

Trans. M. Camillo Camilli and R[ichard] C[arew] Esquire. London: Adam Islip for Thomas Man, 1594.

Iriarte de Aspurz, Lázaro. *Franciscan History: The Three Orders of St. Francis of Assisi.* Chicago: Franciscan Herald Press, 1983.

Jiménez Rueda, Julio. *Sor Juana Inés de la Cruz en su época.* Mexico City: Editorial Porrúa, 1951.

Kagan, Richard L. *Lucrecia's Dream: Politics and Prophecy in Sixteenth-Century Spain.* Berkeley: Univ. of California Press, 1990.

Kamen, Henry. *Spain in the Later Seventeenth Century.* London: Longman, 1980.

Kessell, John L., Rick Hendricks, Meredith D. Dodge, Larry D. Miller, and Eleanor B. Adams, eds. *Remote Beyond Compare: Letters of don Diego de Vargas to His Family from New Spain and New Mexico, 1675–1706.* Albuquerque: Univ. of New Mexico Press, 1989.

Ladd, Doris M. *The Mexican Nobility at Independence, 1780–1826.* Latin American Monographs, 40. Austin: Institute of Latin American Studies, The Univ. of Texas at Austin, 1976.

Larquié, Claude. "Etude de démographie madriléne: La paroisse de San Ginés de 1650 a 1700." *Mélanges de la Casa de Velázquez* 2 (1966).

León, Fr. Luis de. *La perfecta casada.* Madrid: Ruiz Hermanos, Editores, 1917.

León, Nicolás. *La obstétrica en México: Notas bibliográficas, étnicas, históricas, documentarias y críticas, de los orígenes históricos hasta el año 1910*. Mexico City: Tip. de la Vda. de F. Díaz de León, sucrs., 1910.

Leonard, Irving A. *Baroque Times in Old Mexico*. Ann Arbor Paperbacks, 110. Ann Arbor: The Univ. of Michigan Press, 1966.

Lind, James. *Essay on Diseases incidental to Europeans in Hot Climates, with the Method of Preventing Their Fatal Consequences*. Philadelphia: W. Dunne, 1811.

The Liturgy of the Hours According to the Roman Rite. New York: Catholic Book Publishing Co., 1975.

Livermore, H.V. *A Short History of Portugal*. Edinburgh: Edinburgh Univ. Press, 1973.

Livet, G. "International Relations and the Role of France, 1648–60." In *The Decline of Spain and the Thirty Years War, 1609–48/59*. Ed. J.P. Cooper. Vol. 4 of *The New Cambridge Modern History*. Cambridge: Cambridge Univ. Press, 1970.

Loftis, John, ed. *The Memoirs of Anne, Lady Halkett and Ann, Lady Fanshawe*. Oxford: Clarendon Press, 1979.

Lohmann Villena, Guillermo. "Notas sobre el Conde de Cañete, virrey del Perú." *Revista de Indias* 3 (Jul.– Sept. 1942).

Lough, J. "France Under Louis XIV." In *The Ascendency of France, 1648–88*. Ed. F.L. Carsten. Vol. 5 of *The New Cambridge Modern History*. Cambridge: Cambridge Univ. Press, 1961.

Lynch, John. *Spain Under the Habsburgs*. 2d ed . 2 vols. New York:

New York Univ. Press, 1984.

MacLachlan, Colin M., and Jaime E. Rodríguez O. *The Forging of the Cosmic Race: A Reinterpretation of Colonial Mexico.* Berkeley: Univ. of California Press, 1980.

MacLeod, Murdo J. *Spanish Central America: A Socioeconomic History, 1520–1720.* Berkeley: Univ. of California Press, 1973.

Madoz, Pascual. *Diccionario geográfico-estadístico-histórico de España y sus posesiones de ultramar.* 16 vols. Madrid: P. Madoz y L. Sagasti, 1845–50.

Margry, Pierre. *Découverte par mer des bouches du Mississipi et etablissments de Lemoyne D'Iberville sur le Golfe du Mexique, 1694–1703.* Vol. 4 of *Découvertes et établissements des fraçais dans l'ouest en dans le sud de l'Amerique septentrionale, 1614–1754: Mémoires et documents originaux.* Paris: E. Guilmoto, 1876–86.

Marques, António Henrique R. de Oliveira. *History of Portugal.* 2 vols. New York: Columbia Univ. Press, 1972.

Mattingly, Garrett. *Catherine of Aragon.* Boston: Little, Brown and Company, 1941.

Maura y Gamazo, Gabriel, duque de Maura. *Vida y reinado de Carlos II.* 2d ed. 2 vols. Madrid: Espasa-Calpe, 1954.

Mendoza, Vicente T. *Vida y costumbres de la Universidad de México.* Mexico City: Instituto de Investigaciones Estéticas, 1951.

Michaëlis de Vasconcellos, Carolina. *Algumas palavras a respeito de púcaros de Portugal.* Lisbon: Revista "Ocidente," 1957.

Bibliography

Mousnier, R. "French Institutions and Society, 1610–61." In *The Decline of Spain and the Thirty Years War, 1609–48/59*. Ed. J.P. Cooper. Vol. 4 of *The New Cambridge Modern History*. Cambridge: Cambridge Univ. Press, 1970.

Palau y Dulcet, Antonio. *Manual del librero hispanoamericano: Bibliografía general española e hispanoamericana desde la invención de la imprenta hasta nuestros tiempos con el valor comercial de los impresos descritos*. 2d ed. 19 vols. Barcelona: A. Palau, 1948–.

Paz, Octavio. *Sor Juana: Her Life and Her World*. Trans. Margaret Sayers Peden. Cambridge, Mass.: Harvard Univ. Press, 1988.

Paz Soldán, Carlos Enrique. *Las tercianas del Conde de Chinchón (Según el "Diario de Lima" de Juan Antonio Suardo)*. Lima: "La Reforma Médica," 1935.

Pérez Castañeda, María Angeles. *Pruebas para contraer matrimonio con caballeros de la Orden de Santiago*. Madrid: Dirección General del Patrimonio Artístico y Cultural, 1976.

Peterson, Mendel. *Funnel of Gold*. Boston: Little-Brown, 1975.

Phelan, John Leddy. *The Royal Protomedicato: The Regulation of the Medical Professions in the Spanish Empire*. Durham: Duke Univ. Press, 1985.

Picardo y Gómez, Alvaro, ed. *Memorias de Raimundo de Lantéry, mercader de Indias en Cádiz: 1673–1700*. Cadiz: Escelicer, 1949.

Polzer, Charles W., S.J. *Kino Guide II: His Missions, His Monuments*. Tucson: Southwestern Mission Research Center, 1982.

Riley, James C. *Sickness, Recovery and Death: A History and Forecast of Ill Health.* Iowa City: Univ. of Iowa Press, 1989.

Rivera Cambas, Manuel. *Los gobernantes de México: Galería de biografías y retratos de los vireyes, emperadores, presidentes y otros gobernantes que ha tenido México, desde Hernando Cortés hasta el C. Benito Juárez.* Mexico City: Imprenta de J.M. Aguilar Ortiz, 1872–73.

Robles, Antonio de. *Diario de sucesos notables, 1665–1703.* Ed. Antonio Castro Leal. 3 vols. Colección de Escritores Mexicanos, 30–32. Mexico City: Editoral Porrúa, 1946.

Rodríguez Aceves, J. Jesús. *Danzas de moros y cristianos.* Guadalajara: Gobierno de Jalisco, Secretaría General, Unidad Editorial, 1988.

Rosell, Lauro E. *Iglesias y conventos coloniales de México: Historia de cada uno de los que existen en la Ciudad de México.* Mexico City: Editorial Patria, 1979.

Rubio Mañé, José Ignacio. *El Virreinato.* 4 vols. Mexico City: Fondo de Cultura Económica, 1983.

Sabat de Rivers, Georgina. "Sor Juana de la Cruz." In Luis Iñigo Madrigal, coord. *Epoca colonial.* Vol. 1 of *Historia de la literatura hispanoamericana.* Madrid: Ediciones Cátedra, 1982.

Salazar y Castro, Luis de. *Historia genealógica de la casa de Silva.* 2 vols. Madrid: M. Alvarez y M. de Llanos, 1685.

Sánchez Belda, Luis. *Guía del Archivo Histórico Nacional.*

Ediciones conmemorativas del Centenario del Cuerpo Facultativo, 1858–1958, 12. Valencia: Junta Técnica de Archivos, Bibliotecas y Museos, 1958.

Sanz Ayán, Carmen. "Poderosos y privilegiados." In *La vida cotidiana en la España de Velázquez*. Ed. José N. Alcalá-Zamora. Colección Historia, 4. Madrid: Ediciones Temas de Hoy, 1989.

Schäfer, Ernesto. *El Consejo Real y Supremo de las Indias: Su historia, organización y labor administrativa hasta la terminación de la Casa de Austria*. 2 vols. Seville: Centro de Estudio de Historia de América, Univ. de Sevilla, 1935; Seville: Escuela de Estudios Hispano-Americanos, 1947.

Schurz, William Lytle. *The Manila Galleon*. New York: E.P. Dutton & Company, 1939.

Seed, Patricia. *To Love, Honor, and Obey in Colonial Mexico: Conflicts Over Marriage Choice, 1574–1821*. Stanford: Stanford Univ. Press, 1988.

Sigüenza y Góngora, Carlos de. *Alboroto y motín de México del 8 de junio de 1692: Relación de don Carlos de Sigüenza y Góngora en una carta dirigida al almirante don Andrés de Pez*. Ed. Irving A. Leonard. Mexico City: Talleres Gráficos del Museo Nacional de Arqueología, Historia y Etnografía, 1932.

Stradling, R.A. *Europe and the Decline of Spain: A Study of the Spanish System, 1580–1720*. London: George Allen & Unwin, 1981.

Tanguay, L'Abbé Cyprien. *Dictionnaire genealogique des familles canadiennes depuis la fondation de la colonie jusqu'a nos jours*. Quebec: Eusèbe Senécal, 1871.

Tomás y Valiente, Francisco. *Los validos en la monarquía española del siglo xvii: Estudio institucional.* 2d ed. Madrid: Siglo Veintiuno de España Editores, 1982.

Ussel C., Aline. *Esculturas de la Virgen María en Nueva España, 1519–1821.* Mexico City: SEP, Instituto Nacional de Antropología e Historia, Museo Nacional de Historia, 1975.

Uyá, Jaime, ed. *Fuero juzgo o libro de los jueces.* 2 vols. Barcelona: Ediciones Zeus, 1968.

Varey, J.E. "El teatro palaciego y las crisis económicas del siglo xvii." In María Carmen Iglesias, Carlos Moya, and Luis Rodríguez Zúñiga, eds. *Homenaje a José Antonio Maravall.* 3 vols. Madrid: Centro de Investigaciones Sociológicas, 1985.

Vargas Ugarte, Rubén. *Historia del culto de María en Iberoamérica y de sus imágenes y santuarios más celebrados.* Buenos Aires: Editorial Huarpes, 1947.

Vázquez de Prada, Valentín. *Los siglos xvi y xvii.* Vol. 3 of *Historia económica y social de España.* Ed. Valentín Vázquez de Prada. Madrid: Confederación Española de Cajas de Ahorros, 1978.

Vicens Vives, Jaime. *An Economic History of Spain.* Princeton: Princeton Univ. Press, 1969.

Vigil, Mariló. *La vida de las mujeres en los siglos xvi y xvii.* Madrid: Siglo Veintiuno de España Editores, 1986.

Vilar y Pascula, Luis. *Diccionario histórico, genealógico y heráldico de las familias ilustres de la monarquía española.* 8 vols. Madrid: Librería de Don M. Guijarro, 1859–66.

Villaseñor y Villaseñor, Alejandro. *Los Condes de Santiago: Monografía histórica y genealógica*. Mexico City: Tip. de "El Tiempo," 1901.

Vives, Juan Luis. *La mujer cristiana, de los deberes del marido, pedagogia pueril*. Colección Crisol, 59. Trans. Lorenzo Riber. Madrid: M. Aguilar, 1944.

Warman Gryj, Arturo. *La danza de moros y cristianos*. Mexico City: Secretaría de Educación Pública, 1972.

Weddle, Robert S. *Wilderness Manhunt: The Spanish Search for La Salle*. Austin: Univ. of Texas Press, 1973.

Zabaleta, Juan de. *El día de fiesta por la mañana y por la tarde*. Ed. Cristóbal Cuevas García. Clásicos Castalia, 130. Madrid: Editorial Castalia, 1983.

INDEX

INDEX

INDEX

Index

Index

INDEX

Index

INDEX

Index

INDEX

Index

INDEX

INDEX

INDEX

INDEX

Index

INDEX

Index

Two Hearts, One Soul was designed by Harold Augustus
and composed on a Macintosh IIci, using QuarkXpress 3.1
with 11/14 Granjon from the Adobe Type Library.
Outputted on a QMS 1700, laser printer. 600 dpi on
25% Cotton Laser paper.
Printed and bound by Bookcrafters Inc.,
on 60 lb Natural offset.